BEST CANADIAN ESSAYS
2023

BEST
CANADIAN
ESSAYS

2023

EDITED BY
MIREILLE SILCOFF

BIBLIOASIS
WINDSOR, ONTARIO

FIRST EDITION
ISBN 978-1-77196-503-3 (Trade Paper)
ISBN 978-1-77196-504-0 (eBook)

Guest edited by Mireille Silcoff
Copyedited by Emily Donaldson
Cover and text designed by Gordon Robertson

Published with the generous assistance of the Canada Council for the Arts,
which last year invested $153 million to bring the arts to Canadians throughout
the country, and the financial support of the Government of Canada. Biblioasis
also acknowledges the support of the Ontario Arts Council (OAC), an agency
of the Government of Ontario, which last year funded 1,709 individual artists
and 1,078 organizations in 204 communities across Ontario, for a total of
$52.1 million, and the contribution of the Government of Ontario through
the Ontario Book Publishing Tax Credit and Ontario Creates.

PRINTED AND BOUND IN CANADA

CONTENTS

INTRODUCTION

Mireille Silcoff

My biggest question in editing this anthology was Emma Gilchrist. I carried Emma Gilchrist with me in my pocket for weeks, while also carrying around hard copies of *The New Quarterly* and *Brick* and *Canadian Notes & Queries*, along with a growing list of things to read, this hyper-alive list, on my phone, computer, colonizing all spare moments. Ideally, I had to look at every great essay published in a newspaper or periodical or website by a Canadian this year. But until I cracked the Gilchrist question, I'd never be able to do even half that in a decent timeline, because the boundaries would never get hard enough for me to corral the work.

With jobs like this, it's one hundred percent necessary to have some obvious branches that can be chopped. In the past, I've judged big fiction prizes. When you have 120 novels to read, or about ten million words, the books that have sluggish writing in the first ten pages, or accidental bad grammar in the first three, are out. There is so much competition. If an author doesn't have their magnetism or genius or special sauce working by chapter two, they just can't be in the same world of possibility as, say, an Edugyan or Toews. Only a sadistic or insanely Zen judge would call up the will to see if it gets better—not when so many other works get every single thing right from the first word.

Essays are, obviously, shorter than books. An editor doesn't need to be quite so no-soup-for-you. If you get sent something muddy, you can read until the end and see if a diamond or lotus emerges. So I did all that, masked in a west end Montreal café trying to drink coffee and not get over caffeinated, or get Covid, and after months of combing publications, and a disturbing number of Post-it notes and open tabs, I had a giant blob of a number, dozens and dozens. I needed to get that down to fifteen essays. The folks at Biblioasis, this anthology's publisher, were feeling generous and told me that, if I really needed it, I could have sixteen, expecting me to be grateful.

It was then that I *really* had to stop mincing around with cafés and Post-it notes and ask the thing I promised myself I would not ask in this intro: *What is an essay?* If you've read more than a couple of essay anthologies, you will know that it is the rare editor who does not tack their introduction to the clearly irresistible mistral of this question.

As I solidified the list, and got closer to sitting down to write this, I resolved, really resolved, not to do that. I would especially not write about Michel de Montaigne up in his book-lined tower in the late sixteenth century, inventing this new literary genre. I would not write about how an essay—from Montaigne's *essais*—means a trial, a try, a poke in the dark at understanding. Too many have done that already.

But in complete honesty, the question of what a true essay is plagued me through the selection process. The reason I am, with great embarrassment, asking it again, here, is because I've come to realize the definition keeps on subtly changing. The genre, it turns out, is very alive.

For instance, not long ago, even ten years ago, one huge, fashionable concern for the essayist and their critics was the line between fiction and non. If an essayist was writing a personal piece, using composite characters, making up lines and scenes as well as memory allows, boxing reality into good narrative, could it really be called *truth*? After a couple of scandals—James Frey's fake disaster memoir; *New York Times* writers serving 100 percent made-up characters—we saw new literary terms and genres crop up to catch the run-off: "autofiction," the seriously misleading "faction" (*fact* fiction, get it?), "fictionalized memoir," and that sanctimonious gigantopod still eating writing programs whole: the always baggy and forgiving, always softypants-sounding *creative non-fiction*. Remember all those clever subheads playing with the line "based on a true story"?

The creeping vines of fantasy and fabrication were far from a defining concern in editing this year's anthology. If essays can be seen as a marker of zeitgeist, then 2021, the year in which all this book's essays were written, could be called a year of reality check. So much of what I read contained so much zealously backed-up fact that a little bit more fictional wordsong, a touch more poetic license, would have come as *relief*. In short: the realness was *real*.

Which created some confusion. Not least because, at the beginning of the selection process, many publications sent in lists of favourite essays from the year, and fascinatingly, lots of these pieces were not very much essays at all. Often, they felt like lightly reported features—here's a new scientific discovery; here's an interesting political campaign—with a lot of "I" in them. That the first-person has swarmed journalism should not be news to anyone reading this intro (itself swarming with first person). As you might have already noticed, it's increasingly normal now to find a recipe for green goddess dressing or a celebrity profile, or even an investigative piece, with its writer sitting in the middle of it. So many forms of journalism have been made more subjective through a Twitter-informed "this is *my* reality" take on things, the bifurcations of social media cleaving opinion apart to where every writer morphs into their own personal newspaper or magazine—the independent publication called "me."

How interesting, then, that in the more contemplative world of essays, something like the converse has happened. So much personal or ruminative writing has been cannibalized by reportage. This is in no small part the doing of publications afraid to seem non-factual, like they sit anywhere near the liar's court of fake news. This editorial thinking contains a decent amount of fear, if not paranoia. It's not hard to understand. The offendable are everywhere, trigger-happy tweeters lying in wait. All kinds of very vocal camps get irritated and incensed, and so much is hot-button. One can see how a magazine or newspaper or website editor might think, *we need to back everything up all the time now, to stay out of trouble.* I noticed it in my own essay writing this year: I had a couple of editors request more hard fact amid the think, in one case because the magazine's fact checkers had asked for it, in order to keep the piece within the publication's "editorial mandate to educate." Still, the idea that this can only be done with previously corroborated information, content that has been green-lit elsewhere—or that the right *questions* are not sufficient; concrete *answers* must be provided too—seems a chicken-ish game to be playing with a necessarily speculative genre, one which has always been an open field for seminal, or at the very least, original, thought.

The result of all this, in a purely literary frame, is a wide greyspace where this increasingly popular form, the *reported* essay, meets the open fire hydrant of *personal* reportage. For the purposes of this book, only the essay side of this spectrum could be considered. At first, to figure out where a piece fell, I did some idiotic things: I counted quotes, with the idea that if there were more than a couple of outside voices, what I had in my hands was not an essay. I also watched for things like big declarative sentences in introductions, the sort which told you exactly what to expect from the rest of the article, because few essays will do that, while much journalism does. But in the end, these clear cuts were less useful than asking whether a piece was one of interiority (essay) or exteriority (not); a piece of curiosity (essay) or certainty (less so). I needed to feel that a writer was working their way through a skein of ideas and experience, even conflicting, to come to some understanding—even a failed one.

Emma Gilchrist's excellent "Genetic Mapping" was a frontier piece. It crossed the final list's border both ways a few times. First published in *Maisonneuve* magazine, the article is a personal journey, but also contains quite a few quoted sources and straight reporting. It could be called an essay. It could also be called a reported feature. I was, admittedly, very motivated to get it in. Ours is a time where it's increasingly repeated that, at least in the United States, genealogical research is the second most popular hobby, after gardening, and the second most popular search category online, after porn. So there was a giant pile of submissions having to do with ancestry and genetic inheritance. Gilchrist's—which touched on themes of race, DNA testing, the meaning of family, and the fragility of identity—was the one I loved most. I had an image of the man she thought was her dad, sitting across from her in a Nanaimo diner, that would not much fade. It is, without question, great writing. I believe it is great *essay* writing because of Gilchrist's spirit, what could even be called her attitude: she learns as she goes. With every paragraph, she, like the information she receives about her family, is recasting, and finding containers she thought solid to be porous, disintegrating, basically bullshit. By the end of the piece, truth lies everywhere and nowhere at once. This is the wiggly unknowing that often graces the very best essay writing.

The border status of "Genetic Mapping" also appealed, because the idea of boundaries and thresholds crop up in several essays in this anthology. Michelle Good writes about "pretendians" and the need to draw a solid line around what being part of the Indigenous community means; the masterful Kathy Page's affecting "That Other Place" has her with one foot in the world of the well and one in the realm of illness, Allan Stratton writes about what the changing status of the word "trans" means within and outside the queer community, and Paul Howe, a professor at the University of New Brunswick, draws wild lines from the early twentieth-century penning of teens into high school to the ascent of Donald Trump.

Chafic LaRochelle's Essay, "A Man, Without," is a darkly sensitive piece about how war and immigration untethered his father. Kunal Chaudhary's "The Sun Is Always in Your Eyes in Rexdale" painstakingly weaves together how the cloistering of his Toronto neighbourhood by the police, media, and a dunderheaded city hall, created so many of the ills these institutions claimed they were out to cure.

Our current, tumultuous age—which seems to be playing out in hyperspeed—is an important time for essayists, because in moments of great change, it's good to have chroniclers with the presence of mind to step back and assess. Is there ever a day where many of us don't wake up thinking *oh god now what?* anymore? We can all *feel* the gears of change grinding, even if just through the exhaustion of living with their constant squeal. As Tom Rachman points out in his genius essay "Where Is Intellectual Courage in the Age of Twitter?," it's so easy to do fast anger online now. A few essays are here—Good's, Stratton's, Chris Cheung's, on the media's blindness to his Asian American community, and Jamaluddin Aram's searingly sad, almost wailing, "Afghanistan, the Beautiful Land of Endless Suffering"—because their authors chose to lay their fire on the page in one of the most demanding literary genres around, rather than scattering cheap flares in a few characters online. All the above writers are seeing red through their essays, the type nearly burning holes. But none of them are using their voices to dazzle, or to try to get you to like or follow them, or to bully, and make you scared—they are using them sharply and smartly and without remorse, to shake you into listening.

The war in the Ukraine is happening as I write this. Monkeypox has arrived in Canada, Roe v. Wade has just been overturned, and more baldly discriminatory bills are being passed in Quebec. The cost of living is exploding, with every trip to the supermarket checkout laced with more anxiety. I don't know if, by the end of 2022, it will feel like Covid is the runaway problem of the year. But in 2021, the pandemic was still Canada's most defining difficulty and conundrum. From that perch, Stephen Marche examines the changing status of work, Sarmishta Subramanian looks at friendship, and Sharon Butala writes about increased loneliness.

What else can I tell you? Evidently, from the stack of submission I received, Canadians wrote many, *many* essays about fish. I didn't choose any of those. But there is Jane Hu's deceptively charming piece about the Filet-O-Fish, which is here not because it went viral upon publication (it did), but because it contains some subtle magic. After reading it, you will find yourself thinking about her family and the McDonalds sandwich for days. If you are like me, you might even go out and buy a Filet-O-Fish for the first time, to see what it's like.

There was also a huge amount written on trying to get pregnant, being pregnant, and having babies. Heather Jessup's "Klein Bottle" is the representative of this group, and a spectacular outlier too, for meshing complex mathematics with failed novel writing and the workaday surrealism of early motherhood.

I also read a lot of essays that used childhood trauma as narrative motor, the reason everything happens. I found my interest in this newly favourite way of telling a personal story low—if only because the stories can feel so overdetermined. ME Rogan's scalding "Giving Up America," about their abusive childhood, and their choice to ditch their American citizenship, did not, and that's why it is the flag bearer here.

None of the essays you are about to read were selected because they reflect my own politics or my beliefs. There are some that contain views I disagree with, and others I wish I'd written. They are here because in them, I found the writers fully on the page. In our era of thinly thought-through extremity and knee-jerk us vs. them internet thinking, in this time of so much bloodiness and division, I hope this anthology can be a small bid for understanding that a border, a line drawn, need not be only the beginning or the end of something. That a frontier can be a place—indeed is the best place—for a conversation between sides to begin.

GENETIC MAPPING

Emma Gilchrist

On an overcast Sunday morning, one week before Father's Day, I walked inside a breakfast joint in Nanaimo, BC. He was already there waiting for me, wearing his standard outfit: cowboy boots, jean jacket, white hair poking out the back of his cowboy hat. We sunk into a long hug before a server led us to a small booth at the back.

I'd been meeting my biological father in restaurants like this a couple of times a year since we first met sixteen years ago. But this time was different. I was nervous, already starting to sweat beneath my favourite jacket.

Watching him across the table, in a moment I've come to think of as "the before," I tried to memorize every detail of him. His deep olive skin, his kind blue eyes, the dirt beneath his nails. Tears started to cloud my vision, but I blinked them back. We bantered about the pandemic, his wait for shoulder surgery, his non-existent love life. Then he turned the conversation to me.

"I've been yakking too much," he said. "How are you? Have you talked to Kim lately?"

Kim's my birth mom. I knew then that there was no more putting off what I had come here to say. I took a breath, but still had trouble meeting his eyes.

"Yeah, we aren't really talking much these days," I said. "I discovered something I need to tell you."

I had practiced a script for this part, but the tears came before I could get the words out.

"What is it sweetie?" he asked. As the tears turned into sobs, I put my head in my hands. When I finally looked up, our blue eyes locked.

"Guess?" I squeaked out.

"What," he said. "I'm not your dad?"

I nodded. At some point, our breakfast arrived, our eggs growing cold on the plates in front of us.

Scenes like this are playing out for thousands of Canadians thanks to the surging popularity of home DNA testing. Most people signing up for genetic ancestry services like AncestryDNA or 23andMe want to learn more about where their family came from. Others are looking to access information about their health or family medical history, and some are hoping to connect with distant relatives.

But what often starts out as an innocent interest in family history can lead to shocking results, uncovering infidelity, donor conception, adoption and, well, family secrets of all varieties. A whopping 27 percent of DNA test-takers said they learned about close relatives they didn't know about previously, according to a 2019 survey by the Pew Research Center. That's no small number, especially when you consider the fact that 15 percent of US adults have taken a test since the industry launched over a decade ago. (Interest in genetic ancestry testing is growing exponentially: as many people purchased consumer DNA tests in 2018 as in all previous years combined.)

Startling DNA revelations have become so common that 23andMe has dedicated a section on its website to those who discover an "unexpected relationship," directing people in need to a crisis line. "You spit. You waited. And now, you may have discovered something you didn't anticipate," the page says. "23andMe results can reveal new information that has the potential to shift how we think about ourselves and our families." A cottage industry has even sprung up to support people dealing with the explosive fallout of DNA surprises: Facebook groups, books, podcasts and at least one nonprofit.

"Non-paternity events" or "not parent expected" results, as they're crudely called, happen more often than you might think. Within a year of uncovering my own paternity mix-up, I learned of three other people in my social circle who'd recently made similar discoveries through DNA tests. One found out her parents had a threesome and the other man was her true biological father. Another was given a test by her sister for Christmas, only for the "gift" to reveal the news they didn't share a dad. And another learned that her absent father, whose troubled history she was trying to avoid repeating, wasn't her flesh and blood after all.

DNA testing is the latest in a long line of scientific attempts to get a fix on paternity. In the early 1900s, doctors used techniques such as examining dental structures, finger printing and—my personal favourite—measuring noses, according to Nara Milanich, a history professor at Barnard College and author of *Paternity: The Elusive Quest for the Father*. "There's always been this tension between social and biological paternity," says Milanich. "But what genetic science did was lay bare that tension in a way that could previously be ignored or negotiated."

In her book, Milanich writes about Catholic doctors in the mid-1900s who grappled with the moral dilemma of men requesting blood tests for their children because they suspected infidelity. Doctors acted as the gatekeepers of what was seen as the public's "unhealthy curiosity" and often declined such requests.

In the past, paternity secrets might have slipped out through the occasional deathbed confession, whispered conversation, or perplexing blood type result. But the emergence of home DNA testing has done away with gatekeeping and secrecy altogether. "And we never had a conversation as a society about whether that was a good thing or a bad thing," Milanich says. "It just happened."

Suddenly, hundreds of thousands of people are facing the disorienting experience of stumbling upon a biological truth they never went looking for in the first place. That wasn't my experience—at least not exactly. I've always carried questions about who I am and where I'm from. I didn't need to take a DNA test to know that the story of my identity is far from simple. Still, even a lifetime of uncertainty couldn't have prepared me for what happened when I got the results.

In October 1984, my birth mother signed the papers to put me up for adoption in Lethbridge, Alberta. I was five days old.

"She has not seen nor named her baby, stating she chooses not to build an emotional bond with the child," reads the report by the social worker. I spent a few weeks in foster care before two British teachers living in northern Alberta got the phone call they'd been waiting on for years.

My mum scribbled the details of the call furiously on a piece of scrap paper: *Girl. September 30th. Born at noon. Seven pounds seven ounces. Round face. Reddish full head. Plump. Healthy.* They flew south two days later—despite my "reddish full head"—signed the adoption papers, and went home with a new baby.

My parents told me I was adopted from such a young age that I can't remember learning the news for the first time. When I was little, it made me feel special. But as I grew older, curiosity tugged at all corners of me and my mind whirred with the what-ifs. What if my parents had signed up for a baby two weeks later? Would some other little girl be Emma? Would I be someone else? It frightened me to think of how a string of arbitrary events determined who I was.

When I researched adoption laws in Alberta in my teens, I discovered I might never gain access to my own original birth certificate, let alone the names of my birth parents. Every waking moment became shrouded by a string of existential questions: Why am I here? Who was my birth mother? And why did she give me away? *Give me away*. Those were three words I thought about almost constantly.

Juliet Guichon, a medical bioethicist at the University of Calgary, says it's common for adoptees and those conceived through assisted reproductive technologies to start questioning their identities as teenagers. "We are always engaged in identity formation, but the practice is more dominant in our minds during adolescence," she says.

In the mid-1900s, psychologists coined the term "genealogical bewilderment" to refer to the sense of disorientation and disconnection many adoptees experience. Decades of research has shown adoptees and birth parents tend to fare better psychologically under open adoptions, which has helped justify recent changes in adoption practices. "Secrecy is not in the best interests of the child," says Guichon.

The fall I turned eighteen, I moved 600 kilometres south to Calgary. While my friends were excited about going to the bar, I was excited about signing up with Alberta's post-adoption registry. The registry connected adoptees with biological relatives who'd also signed up. I filled out the paperwork, mailed it in and waited. A year went by. Nobody registered.

At that time, the only other option for adoptees looking for answers was to pay to undertake a licensed search through an adoption agency. My parents kindly paid the few hundred bucks to make it happen, and the Alberta government handed over my full adoption file to the agency. (Two years later, in 2004, Alberta followed in the footsteps of BC and Newfoundland by opening adoption records, which means adoptees can access their information once they come of age, unless their biological parents have placed a veto on the file. Most other provinces have since followed suit.)

The agency tracked down my birth mother within a week, even though she'd been living in Mexico for fifteen years. She was eager to connect and immediately signed and faxed a consent form, allowing the agency to release her information to me. When a woman from the agency called me with the news, I scribbled down notes, much like my mum had done for me: *Businesswoman. Loves writing. Yoga and Buddhism. Knows birth father's name.*

I wept happy tears when I got off the phone, then emailed her. I received a response that night.

A little email seems so terribly inadequate, she wrote. *I am thrilled you have found me.*

When I met my birth mother in person, we grabbed each other's freakishly small hands and marvelled at how similar they were. Kim and I shared the same laugh, the same smile, the same mannerisms. We spent two days together in Phoenix, Arizona, a halfway point between our respective homes, trying to catch up on nearly two decades of life. After years of fantasizing about this moment, it passed by in a surreal blur in the desert heat. A few days later, I wrote in my journal that I felt "numb."

Kim had two young children, ran a bustling travel company and was a surfer. She was nineteen when she got pregnant, didn't have a steady boyfriend and didn't feel she had the family support to raise me herself. She told me my birth father's name was Todd. They'd been high school sweethearts in Kimberley, BC, but had broken up by the time I was conceived. He'd known about me since shortly after I was born.

Kim and Todd hadn't spoken in years, but soon after I found Kim, she tracked down a phone number for him. He was living on Vancouver Island and came home from a weekend away to a voicemail with a simple message: "She's here."

I met Todd at Easter dinner at his sister's house in Calgary. His tattoo-covered biceps bulged from his cowboy shirt. He'd lived a rough life—including a brief stint in prison for drug possession—but he was a soft soul and was excited to connect. We searched each other's faces for similarities and found some: our olive skin, our blue eyes, our cheek bones. He was also adopted, which seemed like an uncanny coincidence given I'd only known two other adoptees growing up.

I learned he had Indigenous ancestry. I'd often wondered if the same might be true for me, given I grew up in a northern Alberta town where about 25 percent of the residents were Indigenous. Todd told me he had tracked his Indigenous ancestry all the way back to 1793. His great-great-great-grandfather, Francois Morigeau, lived in BC's Columbia Valley with his Red River Métis wife, Isabella Taylor. They had a son, Baptiste, in the early 1840s who later married Theresa Kaius, a Ktunaxa woman, at St. Eugene Mission. Baptiste was well-known in the area, in part for giving the city of Golden its name.

I studied our family tree and Googled the names of our ancestors, reading articles about their prominent roles within the Métis and Ktunaxa communities. On my twenty-fifth birthday, I drove to the Columbia Valley and visited an elementary school named after Todd's great-uncle and waded in Columbia Lake, imagining my ancestors' toes touching the same stones. I contacted the Windermere Valley Museum, asked for information about our family and received highlighted historical papers in the mail, detailing the colourful history of the Morigeau family.

By this point, I was a young journalist working at a daily newspaper and I was drawn to reporting on environmental issues. Over the next ten years, I travelled with Elders to a spiritual site in northeastern BC and ate sea urchin at a Haisla and Gitga'at feast in Kitamaat Village. I wrote stories about First Nations' fights to save their land from hydro dams, oil development, ski resorts. I took secret comfort in each brush that I had with Indigenous cultures, feeling like I was quietly reclaiming part of my own story.

I had been raised in a white family and experienced all the privilege that comes with that terrain. I knew that even if Todd had Indigenous ancestry—and I did too—I still benefited from whiteness, and nothing would erase that. But being adopted, there was always a blank space in my identity I longed to make sense of. Learning about my birth family's history felt like I was slowly, but surely, filling in the gaps.

In 2011, I got a job on Vancouver Island, where Todd lived. A couple of times a year we'd meet for lunch and excitedly trade notes on what we'd learned about our heritage. We bonded over our shared adoption history and our efforts to reconnect with our biological roots. He'd connected with his birth mother, had attended a family reunion and was chatting online with his Métis cousins. He'd decided he would start using his birth name instead of his adopted name and was planning to apply for Métis citizenship. I hoped to follow in his footsteps and tucked away an application I received in the mail.

Then, in December 2016, the Joseph Boyden scandal broke. As the Canadian author was called out for his shape-shifting statements about his Indigenous ancestry, a sense of unease grew in the pit of my stomach. My father's name wasn't listed on my birth certificate, so on paper I had no connection to him or to my Indigenous ancestry. My close friends knew my story, but I'd never spoken publicly about my history. To reconnect with the Métis community and apply for citizenship, I was going to need proof of our biological connection. And proof doesn't come easily in cases of two generations of adoption.

When ads for consumer DNA tests began popping up in my Facebook feed, it felt like a way to skirt around the awkwardness of asking Todd to take a paternity test. I thought it might help accelerate my research by connecting me with other relatives and confirming my ancestry. So I paid $249 for a kit from 23andMe. It promised to tell me about any health conditions I may have inherited and what percentage of my DNA came from thirty-one populations worldwide, including "Native American."

At the time, I was only vaguely aware of the growing criticisms of genetic ancestry testing led by the Indigenous scholar Kim TallBear, who published a book in 2013 called *Native American DNA: Tribal Belonging and the False Promise of Genetic Science.* "The kind of genetic ancestry tests that people are buying on Ancestry.com don't do very much at all for you," TallBear tells me in an interview. She says Indigenous belonging isn't determined by DNA, but through connections with living people and Indigenous political bodies.

A DNA test "might help you find a biological relative, but you're still going to have to go to the community that has authority over belonging, whether it's political belonging through the form of a First Nation or a band office, or whether it's informal kinship belonging to the family," TallBear says. "You still need to reconnect to somebody and you've still got to show your relationship to living communities."

Recently, a number of high-profile people have had their claims to Indigenous identity called into question after it's been revealed that they have no meaningful connection to a community. In 2019, Elizabeth Warren apologized to the Cherokee Nation for taking a DNA test in an attempt to prove her Native American ancestry. In another controversy reminiscent of the Boyden scandal, in late 2020, Canadian filmmaker Michelle Latimer resigned as the director of CBC's TV series *Trickster* after a CBC investigation alleged that she had claimed false ties to the Kitigan Zibi Anishinabeg First Nation. "Genetic ancestry testing alone is never enough," TallBear tells me. "If it's going to be useful to reconnect, it always has to be coupled with other, more tangible forms of connection."

When I ordered the DNA test, I knew the results would only be one more piece in my identity puzzle. But after having my biological identity hidden from me for much of my life, it felt like a small way to take back control over my own story.

When the box arrived, containing instructions and a test tube, I spit into the tube, slipped it back in the box and popped it in the mail. After a lifetime of fighting for access to my family history, it all felt a little too easy.

Soon after they launched, genetic testing companies started facing criticism over privacy concerns and the way that they categorized people along ethnic lines. But they were also giving adoptees and donor-conceived people fresh hope when it came to finding answers they had long given up on.

BC's Olivia Pratten had spent much of her life fighting for the right of donor-conceived people to know their biological origins. In the BC Supreme Court, Pratten argued that people conceived through an anonymous sperm donor, like herself, should have the same rights as adopted people in the province (adoptees in BC became the first in Canada to gain access to their own records in 1995). In May 2011, the BC Supreme Court ruled in Pratten's favour, saying people who are deprived of their genetic backgrounds suffer psychological harm. But the BC government appealed the ruling and won in 2012.

Pratten, who's now thirty-eight, says she thought she'd made peace with not knowing who her biological father was. But just as her court battle ended, home DNA testing happened to be becoming more accessible. She was living in Toronto at the time and Ancestry wasn't shipping kits to Canada yet, so she had a kit shipped to Buffalo, New York, and drove across the border to pick it up. She checked the database once a week for four years, hoping that a match in the system would reveal her biological identity. Then one day in 2017, it happened.

Pratten tells me that discovering the identity of her biological father was complicated, but it also came as a relief. "I waited thirty years for this," she says. "I should not have had to wait this long. I could literally feel the mental weight . . . lift from me instantly."

Pratten, who also learned she was Jewish via the DNA test, said not being able to answer doctors' questions about her family medical history had become extremely upsetting to her. "There was something about not knowing for that long that felt degrading and it's only with hindsight that I can see that now," she says. "There's dignity in knowing."

All of the donor-conceived people who fought alongside Pratten for over a decade have now found answers through DNA testing, she says. "No one can promise anonymity anymore in Canada. DNA testing has completely usurped all the power and authority of the clinics and I completely celebrate it," she says. "There's no conversation anymore about whether you have the right to know."

Of course, one person's right to know impacts another person's right to privacy. But province after province has decided the right of a child to know their biological history comes first—at least in cases of adoption. Anonymous sperm donation has been outlawed in Australia, New Zealand and much of Europe, but is still legal in Canada.

Within a year of finding out her biological origins, Pratten was pregnant with her first child. She thinks there was something on a subconscious level holding her back from starting a family until she'd found her own answers. "He'll never know the mystery that I had to deal with," she says of her son. "He will have answers about his ancestry and knowledge about that from the day he was born."

My own DNA results arrived two months after I spit in the tube. I clicked them open right away, impatient to learn the truth. Staring at the colour-coded world map in front of me, I learned that the test didn't detect any "Native American" ancestry at all. Instead, the pie chart said I was 23.9 percent southern European, mostly Spanish and Portuguese. I was shocked, my head swimming with possibilities.

I hoped there had been a mix-up—that maybe somewhere along the line there had been a mistake in Todd's paternity, but that he was still my father. Luckily, by coincidence, Todd had purchased a genetic ancestry test just three days before I had ordered mine. He had gone with a different company, AncestryDNA, and would have his results soon.

When they came in, I nagged him to send me a screenshot, careful not to let on why I was so anxious to see them. His map didn't match mine in puzzling ways. I saw that he had Native American and Nordic ancestry, while I had none.

Still, I didn't want to jump to conclusions. I had heard that testing through different companies could render different results. (A CBC investigation in 2019 revealed identical twins received significantly different ancestry estimates even when testing with the same company. 23andMe attributed the difference to their algorithm and pointed to the fact that its results are "statistical estimates.") I decided to order a test through the same company as Todd. Surely, I figured, the database would match us as family members.

But another train of thought had started unravelling in my mind like a runaway spool of wool. I messaged my birth mom—whom I'd seen a few times over the years and stayed in regular contact with—to tell her about my surprising Portuguese ancestry and ask if there'd been someone else. *Definitely no other candidate*, she replied.

I received a cheery email with my results in late September 2017: *Great news! Your AncestryDNA results are in.*

But it wasn't great news. Todd and I weren't matched. The man I'd spent fourteen years building a relationship with on the basis of a biological connection wasn't related to me at all.

For months, I felt like a stowaway on a cargo ship pulling away from land, everything I thought I knew fading into the distance. How could it be that these things I'd believed my entire adult life, that had informed so much of who I'd become, were untrue?

In those early days, I couldn't even bring myself to share the news with my partner or closest friends. Three months after I received the results, I was 6,000 kilometres from home on a roadless island in Panama when I divulged my secret for the first time to a couple I'd just met. "I realized I just didn't want it to be real," I wrote in my journal after my confession. "There's some kind of cruelty to this being the end of my story—to this secret being the brick wall, the end of the road, to have my identity concealed from me not once, but twice."

Brianne Kirkpatrick, a genetic counsellor who specializes in coaching people who have discovered family secrets, says she's noticed similarities between the experiences of adoptees and those who discover non-paternity events. "It's the experience of being treated as a perpetual child," Kirkpatrick says. "You're denied rights to your own birth history, rights to your own genetic identity." She says discovering your biological father isn't who you thought he was is a traumatic experience for many people and often provokes grief, which can strain relationships.

When a DNA surprise comes to light, it doesn't just implicate the person who has made the discovery. The grief ripples out, intensifying an already destabilizing experience. "DNA is not only my information. It's my siblings' information, it's my children's information, it's my parent's information," says Françoise Baylis, a professor of bioethics and philosophy at Dalhousie University. "Up until this point when we've done work with DNA, we've asked for informed consent." But now you don't even have to be the one taking the test to risk having your life changed by the results.

I decided not to break the news to Todd at first. I was his only child and I couldn't bear the thought of his heartache. Besides, who knew if I'd ever find my actual biological father?

Why hurt an innocent person for nothing? If I had to live with this lie, I would. But there was a great ache inside of me.

Six months later, I received an email from Ancestry about a new DNA match. A man named Chad who lived in Vancouver was listed as my first or second cousin. I was quite certain he wasn't from my mom's side of the family, so I tracked him down on Facebook and sent him a message. I was working twelve-hour days at the time, and didn't give it much thought as the months passed and Chad didn't see my message.

But on the last day of 2019, more than a year after I sent the note, Chad replied and we started chatting. I told him about my Portuguese ancestry and he mentioned that he had some Portuguese cousins. I told him my birth mother was from Kimberley. He replied that his aunt had lived in Cranbrook, just a twenty-five minute drive away. When he wrote that I actually looked like some of his cousins, my heart sped up. We agreed to meet for coffee the next time he visited Vancouver Island.

A couple months later, before that coffee date could happen, I received a message request on Facebook from a guy named Shawn Mendes. The note said he'd been chatting with his cousin, Chad.

Based on the story he told me, he wrote, *I suspect we may be related.*

I asked Shawn where he went to high school and how old he was.

Cranbrook, he typed. *Fifty-five.*

Then I asked him if he knew Kim.

That's a name I have not heard for a very long time, he wrote. How do you know her?

She's my birth mother, I replied. *Were you romantically involved?*

Kim was the first girl I was ever that romantically involved with. A short relationship. January '84. Were you by chance born in October '84?

Woah, I typed. *I was born September 30, 1984.*

Oh my god, he wrote. *My heart is racing.*

After decades of searching for my biological truth, it ultimately took just fourteen minutes to unravel the mystery.

"I feel like it's a first date," Shawn said when we talked on the phone the next morning. "I'm a bit nervous."

He told me about his dalliance with my birth mother, which he remembered vividly since it was his first time *ever* having sex. Their brief relationship just kind of ended, like many teenage romances do. Shawn went travelling in Europe and then moved to Vancouver. He remembered running into Kim at a festival in Kimberley about six months later when she was visibly pregnant. "When she saw me she just said, in a very convincing fashion, 'It's not yours.'"

Given travel restrictions due to Covid-19, my relationship with Shawn blossomed over text. We couldn't believe our similarities. He was a climate policy nerd. I ran an environmental magazine. He lived in Stockholm. I lived in Stockholm a few years back. We were both news junkies. Avid travellers. Adventure seekers. He makes me feel more *me*.

It was as if I'd been fumbling around in a dark room most of my life, occasionally bumping into sharp objects. And then, in my thirty-sixth year, someone flicked the lights on.

I called Kim to tell her that Shawn and I had found each other. My palms were sweating, worried about how she might react, but she didn't miss a beat.

"Oh my God, Emma, he's your dad," she said. "I've got tingly feelings all over. I totally remember his blue eyes. I remember the space between his front teeth and his dimples." My blue eyes. My gap. My dimples.

I hadn't expected her to remember Shawn so readily, given she'd said there were no other dad candidates. When I hung up, I felt like I had more questions than answers.

Shawn and I agreed he should take a DNA test, just so we could be sure. The results confirmed what I already felt certain was true. The site told me I shared 49.6 percent of my DNA with him, which suggested *the following estimated relationship: father*.

The more Shawn and I connected, the more I grieved what we'd missed. I recast my entire adult life, wondering how it would have unfolded differently if I'd known him sooner. I created a Mendes album on my phone, with photos of Shawn and his family, including a new half-sister and brother who were twelve and fourteen at the time.

I learned about my Portuguese grandfather, who was one of twelve children born and raised in Trinidad, before immigrating to Labrador in the fifties. Shawn described him as a "viciously progressive" man who rode his bike to work at a coal mine. He told me about my grandmother, one of fourteen children born in Newfoundland. Luckily, they were both still alive and living in BC.

Suddenly, it all felt so obvious: my four trips to Portugal. My three Portuguese boyfriends, despite only 1.4 percent of Canadians claiming Portuguese ancestry. My ex's Portuguese aunt asking if I was *sure* I wasn't Portuguese. My dedication to drinking only vinho verde. The Portuguese lessons on my phone. My obsession with the Portuguese word *saudade*, which can be roughly translated to a nostalgic longing to be near again to something or someone that's been loved and lost, with the knowledge that it or they may never return.

I was left wondering how much of my past can be explained by my biology. Was my feeling of *saudade* always leading me back to the ancestral land of my grandfather?

Wendy Roth is a University of Pennsylvania sociologist who researches how genetic ancestry tests impact consumers' racial and ethnic identities. She tells me there's a name some people use for the pull I described. "It's called blood memory. It's this idea that somehow your genes or your blood sort of know what your ancestry is and leads you to it," she says. "But is there any evidence to support it? No, there isn't."

Roth says my experience is not uncommon among test-takers and is probably better explained by psychology. "You're now looking back on past experience through this particular lens, trying to look for every piece of evidence to suggest Portuguese interest that you've ever had in your life," she says. When I believed my biological father had Indigenous ancestry, she noted, I thought that made sense, too. "You sort of look for the facts or pieces of information that help you to make sense of the new finding."

While the spiritual side of me wants to believe there are things science can't explain, Roth warns the concept of "blood memory" is dangerous. "The idea that it's possible to even have blood memory suggests there is something different about a person's blood or a person's DNA or a person's biology that is connected to being part of a group that we call 'ethnic' or that we call 'racial.'" That implies that ethnicity and race are based in genetics, when in fact they're social constructs. "It feels almost mystical or magical, but it's got this dark underbelly, which is that it reinforces a lot of really dangerous views."

As an adoptee, I get that genetics aren't everything. I know the love my parents and I share for one another is not any less than the love shared between biological parents and their children. I adored my British grandparents despite sharing no biological connection with them whatsoever. But surely there's got to be room in our understanding of ourselves that allows nature to have at least some influence over who we become?

"I do believe there is a nature side to our personalities," Roth says. "There is a profound connection we have to the people that we are descended from." But while this biological connection may be real, it's not organized around ethnic or racial lines. In other words, I might feel a profound bond to my new Portuguese grandpa, but that doesn't mean I'm tied to all Portuguese people. (Though one study did find that people are subliminally attracted to features of their opposite-sex parent—which might explain all those Portuguese boyfriends.)

Crucially, Roth explains that discovering a new ethnic background through a DNA test does not automatically change a person's ethnicity. Ethnicity is shaped by culture, traditions and family connections, not biology. Despite this reality, her research has found that white people are the most likely among test-takers to change their ethnic or racial identities after they receive unexpected ancestry results. This is in part because Black and Latino identities have always been thought of as multiracial. But Roth has also noticed that white people are often looking for "a sense of belonging."

Much like false claims to Indigenous identities, this pattern raises all kinds of ethical questions: In what ways could white people stand to benefit from shifting their ethnic or racial identities? How could this harm people of colour? How will this trend reinforce problematic understandings of the relationship between race and biology? White people taking DNA tests need to grapple with these questions.

Roth's research doesn't map neatly on to my experience, because it doesn't focus on the uniquely disorienting experience of people who have discovered new biological fathers, or on adoptees. Here's what I know to be true: in the absence of other forms of information, DNA tests can be a lifeline for people who've been disenfranchised by government systems that serve to separate children from their biological families. I shouldn't have ever had to fight for access to my own birth information, but I did—and a DNA test ended up playing a crucial role in my journey to piece together the truth of where I came from.

Nine months after finding Shawn, I sat down at my desk one morning and saw a tribute he'd posted to my grandfather, Joseph Concepção Mendes, on his ninety-second birthday. *Born in Trinidad in 1928, he has celebrated birthdays in eleven decades. He has never been a fan of norms and rules, but it would be hard to find a person with a more creative mind or with a stronger moral compass.*

Tears streamed down my face. This man, whom I felt like I've been drawn to like a magnet across time and space, now had dementia and was locked in a care home during the pandemic. I could have known him for at least sixteen years. We'd never get that time back. I'd never get the chance to know my Grandpa Mendes, nor him me. I'm not a religious person, but I found myself praying that I could lay eyes on him, that I could hear his voice, even just once.

In the dappled light of Vancouver Island's old-growth trees, I hiked down a steep trail with Kim and pushed her for answers. She slipped a couple of times and looked fragile, like a young deer just getting its legs. It was September 2020, and I had spent the past six months trying to put together a timeline, desperate to understand how I ended up with the wrong biological father for all of my adult life.

I had already cross-examined Kim, Todd and Shawn over the phone, and even reached out to the boyfriend Kim was with during most of her pregnancy. He'd responded once before going dark. It was unclear why, but Kim claimed not to remember much from the time around my conception. She said she hadn't discovered she was pregnant until she was six months along. She never had an ultrasound, so her due date was a month off.

While she remembered dating Shawn briefly, she had no memory of running into him when she was pregnant in the summer of 1984. "I didn't consider him a candidate. He was a really nice guy. I would have told him," she said. "Nothing made sense. If anything had made sense, I maybe wouldn't have given you up for adoption."

After everything, it seemed my misattributed paternity came down to foggy memories and no one bothering to do the math. I was exhausted and frustrated, but mostly sad—for me, for Todd, for Shawn. The emotional rollercoaster was made worse by the fact that there isn't a playbook for this type of event. When someone loses a parent, people know how to act. But no one knows how to respond when you find out you aren't who you thought you were. There are no sick days or compassionate leave.

For months, I felt as though I was watching life unfold through a frosted window. I could see everyone carrying on with their lives on the other side, but I was in a fog.

Guichon, the bioethicist from the University of Calgary, says recreating an identity after a paternity surprise is a psychologically wrenching process. "People have built their lives on a certain premise and that premise is now gone. They have to create a whole new understanding of who they are and who their people are," she says. "It's real work. Society doesn't recognize what you're going through."

These feelings were complicated by the fact that while I was angry I'd been prevented from knowing the most basic facts about myself for three decades, I also felt sorry for Kim.

In her therapy practice, Kirkpatrick has noticed patterns in how biological mothers respond to paternity surprises. "Some of the stories are probably the truth. And some are probably trying to protect themselves or their reputation, or holding onto a lie that they've worked so hard to keep. They're afraid that everything is going to fall apart if that lie gets exposed," she says. "It's hard to judge people in the past when you don't know what the culture was like around that person. Maybe if they were living in today's time they would have made a different choice."

After our visit, Kim sent me a text: *I truly am so deeply sorry and I know it is pretty irreparable.*

I told her I'd love an explanation someday, but was open to accepting it doesn't exist. For my own sake, I needed to start letting go of my anger. I tried to focus on being grateful for the fact that, against all odds, Shawn and I found each other, and with any luck we'd now get the chance to make up for lost time. But before that could happen, I knew I had to tell everyone the truth—including the person it would hurt the most.

Tucked in the booth at the back of the diner, after I sputtered out the news, Todd said he felt empty. Despite his rough cowboy exterior, he was visibly shaken. "I was really looking forward to having grandchildren, to getting them up on the horses," he said.

He slipped away to the washroom for a while after that. When he came back, he pulled up a photo from my wedding last fall—the two of us are smiling from ear to ear. "That's one of my favourite photos," he said.

I sat outside the restaurant sobbing in my truck after. I felt wrung out, a lifetime's worth of struggle culminating in this one excruciating morning. Todd and I saw each other several times over the next few months, pulled closer together by the fear of how this news might alter us.

"In my heart of hearts you are my daughter," he told me, a few months later. "I never questioned it because I wanted it so badly. I still do." Even so, he said he knew the truth right away that day. "It was just a look in your eyes."

"Father's intuition," I replied.

A year after discovering a new biological father, I'm still working on finding my balance. Once it's safe to travel again, I plan on making new memories. Shawn and I message constantly about possible plans: first up, meeting my grandparents, then visiting Madeira, Trinidad, Newfoundland.

In the meantime, here's what I know for sure: I have three fathers who love me. One is my true dad—the man who raised me and has always told me "the more people who love you the better." One has the softest heart and shares my experience of being adopted. And one feels like a soulmate even though we've never met.

WHERE IS INTELLECTUAL COURAGE IN THE AGE OF TWITTER?

Tom Rachman

His glasses are crooked. So is his smile.

The intellectual has posed too long, looking into a camera lens when he'd rather look into a book. He seems familiar, this fellow in his thirties, perhaps from the glossy jacket of a dull volume. Or, if you attend such events, he's glimpsed at a literary launch, distracted because his phone beeps—he must tweet something quickly, then is back, attention elsewhere, thinking of words.

But, no. The man in this photo is an intellectual of an earlier age, Leone Ginzburg, a literary luminary raised in Mussolini's Italy.

By the age of 19, he had translated Anna Karenina, and would've enjoyed a professor's career. But he refused to pledge allegiance to the Fascist Party, joining the resistance instead.

The authorities imprisoned him for two years, and exiled him to the mountains of Abruzzo during the Second World War. Fittingly, he spent his confinement working on a translation of War and Peace.

When Mussolini's regime fell in 1943, Ginzburg hastened to Rome. So did Hitler's troops. As they swarmed the city, he published a clandestine paper, *L'Italia Libera*. Men burst into the makeshift newsroom. Ginzburg, a Jew, found himself in the custody of Nazis. At a hulking prison on the Tiber, they brutalized him.

A fellow inmate long remembered Ginzburg's warning after an interrogation. "Heaven help us if we're unable to forget our suffering," he said, still bleeding. "Heaven help us if we visit this same punishment on the German people."

That is courage.

The unpleasant facts

Each generation is supplied with a similar proportion of bold outsiders and timid conformists. But circumstances change, thrusting certain personalities to prominence, assigning others to obscurity. Today, Ginzburg might have been lecturing in a college town, perhaps under Covid-19 lockdown at a modest apartment, seated before the silver MacBook, crooked glasses and crooked smile on a Zoom call.

Nowadays, the West is far from its twentieth-century totalitarian nightmare. Yet these are testing times. The power of facing unpleasant facts, as George Orwell put it, remains critical to decency, to sanity, to our health. But where is intellectual courage in the age of Twitter?

Even avid Twitter users dub the platform a hellscape, with its dog-piles and dunks and moral grandstanding. In one respect, it's hopeful that we fight over what amounts to good and evil online. Places where intellectual bravery is indisputable are places to avoid: All you'd need to test your courage in Pyongyang is one wrong sentence. Those endless disputes on Twitter are also the din of free speech.

And, like it or not, Twitter is where the intelligentsia gathers, where the cultural conversation resounds. Academics and journalists, artists and activists—they're all tweeting. It's the greatest intellectual forum in human history (provided that "greatest" is understood only as "largest").

Would Orwell be on Twitter? The question saddens me. For he would.

Twitterphobia

Whenever I learn of a hot new app, I think, "Who would want that?" Typically, the answer is several billion of us. This is why I'm not a venture capitalist, or part of why.

The first tweet was sent by the company's co-founder, Jack Dorsey, on March 21, 2006. When I first heard of the platform the following year, it sounded ludicrous: San Francisco bores chirping about what they'd grab for lunch. This app let you send text messages in public, but I'd never stream a phone call online for all to hear. Why would I tweet?

So I snubbed Twitter, much as you spurn the popular kid who isn't aware of your existence.

For years, I got away with it. I had quit a newspaper job at the end of 2008 to write fiction. Back then, publishers were delighted if an author arrived with legions of followers, but it wasn't mandatory. They merely nudged me to tweet, and when I declined, they smiled: Ah, writers and their misanthropic ways!

Meantime, my former newsroom colleagues found themselves saddled with an extra part-time job, tweeting. Journalistic outfits that once expected reporters to guard scoops now wanted them blurted. Attracting Twitter followers was best achieved through edgy quips and extreme opinions—the precise formula, it turned out, for getting fired.

During the ensuing tumult, I retained the luxury of a delete key, compiling my thoughts in private, discarding most, publishing what remained in 350-page chunks, thrice a decade.

I avoided Twitter with scorn and with fear, if those aren't the same thing. I had more dignified reasons, too. In loud rooms, my inclination is not to raise my voice, but to leave. Also, I cherish my privacy. So I shrank from a life moderated by the ghost-presence of an online audience. Otherwise, I feared, I would never quite be there at dinner, wondering how to phrase the zinger in my head for the scores who weren't present, those whom I'd never dine with but whose numbers far outranked the few looking at me across the table.

More to the point, I never had anything to tweet. This mystified me. I am overstuffed with opinions, and I'd sought a career in writing. But to Twitter, I had nothing to declare. It felt immodest, like shouting my opinions on a bus. I had tweeter's block.

Nor did front-line reports tempt me. On Twitter, they said, hecklers hold the stage and the earnest become self-righteous. I'd sit out this fad. Only, it didn't pass. But the years did, and I watched the intellectual world drift away. Novels were dwindling in relevance—something I mourned, and still do. I grew anxious.

I started lurking on Twitter, dismayed both at politics on the right and culture on the left. My intellectual heroes had always spoken in public, no matter the bullies. But what should I declare? Then, a few days after Donald Trump's loss, I tweeted for the first time, a sign of relief and optimism: "Cannot wait to read the inside story of Trump as he absorbed the news #USElection2020." I'd said nothing notable, just a throat-clearing before a crowd of none.

Or next to none. For someone noticed, a friend who immediately messaged me, "Prepare to have your life ruined."

What *is* intellectual bravery?

The week of the 9/11 attacks, Susan Sontag wrote a reaction, describing courage as a morally neutral virtue. "Whatever may be said of the perpetrators of Tuesday's slaughter," she remarked, "they were not cowards." This opinion—as the rubble still smoldered—was not greeted with cheers. Nobody understands "courageous" as a neutral virtue. It's shorthand for "heroic."

If intellectual courage were about challenging established views because you deem it just, and doing this irrespective of risk, we'd have to define as brave those who call Covid-19 a hoax. And Holocaust deniers, too—they voice unpopular opinions at a heavy social cost. On the other side, take Greta Thunberg. Right-wing commentators taunt her, but she is hardly challenging prevailing views. Nor is she punished for speaking. She is lavished with awards. But who—Covid-19 crackpot or Greta Thunberg—would you rather call courageous?

Intellectual courage means offending mainstream opinion in a way that mainstream opinion will eventually endorse. Martin Luther King Jr and Mary Wollstonecraft and Mahatma Gandhi—morally, they got there first. This points to a problem of intellectual courage in the age of Twitter: What is mainstream opinion? Is it what led to Donald Trump and Boris Johnson? Or Justin Trudeau and Angela Merkel? Is it mainstream to support Black Lives Matter? Or to support Jordan Peterson?

The elusiveness of intellectual courage derives from this: "the culture" does not exist any more. It's subcultures all the way down, most evidently on Twitter, each clan affirming its own rectitude—while hurling Molotov cocktails over the wall at its chosen sinners. Those wounded in such strikes may be shocked at the explosions. But a bomb attack is rarely about the victim; it's a loyalty display.

By now, the traditional left/right divide is mainly tribal. A more intriguing split is between authoritarian and liberal. And those (on the left and right) with authoritarian tendencies are closer in spirit than they admit, whether religious fundamentalists trying to silence comedians who offend, or woke activists using moral blackmail against those who question their worldview, or Republican congressmen conniving to expunge votes they don't like. Each is a marriage of the power-craving opportunist and the genuinely scared.

Presumably, you could demonstrate intellectual courage by breaking with the orthodoxy of your subculture. But even this fails. Immediately, you'd be flung over the wall into the opposing tribe. That is why liberals have been paralyzed in recent years: troubled by the excesses of wokeness, but aghast at being associated with the opposite clan, where one's welcome-hug might come from the likes of Donald Trump Jr.

Is courage even possible on Twitter?

Who hasn't blared an opinion among acquaintances only to have someone introduce heaps of contrary evidence, debunking your assertion. Did you recant? The very confident will have, and the very insecure. But the mass of us— those who oscillate between egotism and self-doubt—may recall times when we insisted on a claim merely because it had barged through our lips. We left that party or that classroom, and in another setting, where nobody knew what we'd said, we asserted the opposite view.

But stupid opinions are indelible on Twitter. You may delete them, but this only draws attention to the blunder. To tweet is to cover yourself in tattoos. Your style may change, but you're stuck with that butterfly on your lower back. Worse, you condemn yourself to repetition, forcing the future-you to keep defending a past-you. Self-expression becomes the enemy of wisdom.

"I don't think the problem with the internet is that we now live in bubbles," the French-Moroccan journalist Marie Le Conte wrote (on Twitter). "I think the problem with the internet is that we're all together, all the time, and that's not something humans are built for. We're not made to be constant; people will always change what they say, and how they say it, depending on who they're talking to, not because they're two-faced but because we're inherently social and that means adapting ourselves to who's in front of us."

We're skittish little creatures, evolved over millennia, thrown online without the wherewithal to cope. Tech algorithms burrow into our limbic systems, feeding off primitive arousal. People may have wisdom to impart; people don't have equal nervous systems. And I still don't know what to tweet.

Is Twitter a mass-delusion?

Four of every five people questioned in a US study said they didn't even use Twitter[1]. Among those who did, the users obsessing about politics were a bubble within a bubble: You'd approach 49 Americans who weren't tweeting feverishly about this stuff to find the one who was.

I've certainly met important figures who didn't bother with Twitter. And I know other people—including many of the most courageous—who would never tweet.

Yet it does matter, this addictive, distressing influence machine. Even if the prudent stay clear, this is where the intelligentsia pushes and pulls at ideas, the brilliant ones amid the preposterous. Never is it certain which will take over the world.

What's sure is this: That which changes society was once just a notion in a lonely mind, uttered passionately to a few who first frowned—then stopped frowning. Wishing away the ills of the internet is fruitless. This is what our generation has.

Only, I don't know who's in control of it all. When Twitter banned Trump this month, the company exhibited all the courage of a wealthy gent who—after watching revolutionaries hang the tyrant—rushes forth to fire bullets into the corpse, all while proclaiming himself on the right side of history.

The silence of Mr Trump has been a blessed relief. But debate grows louder over whether private companies should control public speech. I wonder, though, how much they really control any more. A half-billion tweets come out daily. It's folly to imagine moderators sifting through them, evaluating which are hate speech, which are sarcasm. Supposedly, the answer is to use artificial intelligence. But this would mean training machines on the principles of verbal harm, balance and wit. Humans have yet to agree on any of those.

To tweet? Or not to tweet?

Among my worries about joining Twitter was that its tentacles would intrude into my offline existence. But "offline" hardly exists today. For many of us, experience comes first via the internet (work, socializing, entertainment, humour, politics). We undertake digital-detox regimens and special vacations to visit the old world, the unconnected one. Even then, the prospect of a few days offline, let alone a week, is attended with awe, even alarm.

And I still can't bring myself to tweet. Perhaps it's my upbringing. Perhaps it's cowardice. Yet cowardice is not anyone's permanent condition. Bravery can be a single act; you might wait a lifetime to meet the opportunity. Equally, bravery may be private, an act that doesn't merit retweeting: for example, summoning courage enough to find humanity in those who wound you.

Returning to that prison cell, Leone Ginzburg said: "Heaven help us if we're unable to forget our suffering. Heaven help us if we visit this same punishment on the German people."

We are not tortured by Nazis today, even if the overblown rhetoric on Twitter might make it seem so. Our courage is of a far, far lower order than that of Ginzburg, or of those in torture cells right now as you read this. We are overloaded with places to speak. That does not mean we must shout. Nor, when hearing others' din, should we retreat.

A measured thought, uttered with honesty, even if heard only by a few, asserts a dignity that the intelligentsia can embody again, must embody again.

"Freed from fear"

Ginzburg never read another book after the age of 34. He wrote no great work, never became a grand figure of politics. But we remember the courageous for a reason. Courage is infectious, just as cowardice has been in recent years.

Ginzburg lay in the prison infirmary on Feb 4, 1944, trying not to dwell on his three young children—the separation was excruciating. But thoughts of his wife, Natalia, emboldened him. The lightbulb above his bed was too far away and too dim, so he wrote blind, unable to see these words:

"In recent times I have been thinking about our life together. Our only enemy (I concluded) was my fear. The times that I, for some reason, was assailed by fear, I concentrated all my faculties so much to overcome it and not fail in my duty, that I had no force left. Isn't that so? If and when we meet again, I will be freed from fear, and even these dark areas will no longer exist in our life together.... Kiss the children. I bless all four of you, and thank you for being in the world."

He died a few hours later, never knowing that his wife, Natalia Ginzburg, was to become one of the great Italian novelists, nor witnessing the victories of his three children. Before writing his name in the darkness, he signed off this way:

"Be brave."

Notes

1   https://www.pewresearch.org/politics/2019/10/23/national-politics-on-twitter-small-share-of-u-s-adults-produce-majority-of-tweets/

"PLAY INDIANS" INFLICT REAL HARM ON INDIGENOUS PEOPLE

Michelle Good

As a child, I often saw young settler kids playing at being Indian, replete with pleather headbands, multicolour feathers and plastic tomahawks. Of course, how could the game be played without the cowboys? All the kids wanted to be cowboys. Who could blame them? The Indians always ended up dead in pretend burnings, hangings, beatings, shootings and other inventive executions. However, the "Indians" were always stoic and noble, even when facing their dreadful demise. It was baffling to me. None of my Indigenous relations looked or behaved like that. Now I understand it differently. Little settler kids were giving life to the colonial history they learned in school and the ubiquitous myth of the noble savage. Just so, the hallmark of the Play Indian is an overblown, Hollywood-esque idea of Indigenous knowledge, not to mention the visual trappings—costumes, tattoo identification art, feathers and such.

There are settlers who just won't give up playing Indian. With the drive to Indigenize the academy and for industry to have an Indigenous presence in their consultation processes, some of these imposters come to occupy places and positions that should be occupied by Indigenous people. The arts are no exception. The problem is not only that these Pretendians are asserting themselves in places they have no right to be; they are promulgating yet another round of fabricated history, transferring the mantle of the noble savage to a new genera-tion of Play Indians.

This is an act that transcends the individual. This is about a colonial imperative that works against us just as all the other implements in the colonial toolkit work against us. Playing Indian and following the settler script of what "Indian" means is no different and no less harmful than any other colonial effort to apply a settler overlay on everything Indigenous; to create us in their own image and to expect our collaboration in their effort to do so. Just as church and state collaborated in their assimilation and termination plans, the Play Indian's promul-gation of made-up ideas about Indigeneity works in concert with modern society's toleration of and government inaction regarding everything from the continuing quest for justice for our Murdered and Missing Indigenous Women and Girls to the wholesale apprehension and warehousing of Indigenous children to the absence of potable water in many Indigenous communities, and many other items on that long, long list.

This false image of Indigeneity arises from the fact that these people are not Indigenous. True, they might run a DNA test and find that somewhere in the annals of history a soup-con of Indigenous blood is noted. But blood quantum is not how Canada (or Indigenous peoples, for that matter) define Indigeneity. Rather, in Canada, to be legally recognized as an Indian, a person must meet a legislated definition. By the contortions of the relevant sections of the *Indian Act*, Indians are defined in Canada as those who meet the conditions set out therein. Too many Indigenous people have failed and continue to fail to meet the requirements of the Act in terms of what it means to be a registered Indian. These people can then be legally denied membership in First Nations communities, and with that they are denied the right to participate in their own community affairs. If Indigenous persons who know their own

genealogy going back generations can still be denied legal recognition of their Indigeneity, shouldn't these play actors be held
to a commensurate standard when they claim to be Indigenous? Shouldn't they also be required to produce a painstakingly
accurate family history to warrant calling themselves Indigenous? Something beyond a tiny spike on a DNA test?

These Play Indians express tenuous links, often to a single,
solitary Indigenous person from hundreds of years ago. That
kind of weak historical link does not create a right to identify
as being of the Indigenous community. For example, consider my circumstance as a person of mixed blood. I have one
Indigenous parent; the other is French and English. Let's say
some genealogical history is undertaken, and it's discovered
that there's a 600-year-old paternal link to the British Royal
Family. Can I call myself a royal? Am I entitled to be considered
a member of the community the Royal Family comprises? Of
course not. And why? Because being a member of a community is much more than finding a blood link from long ago.

In the world of the social scientist, the idea of what community
means is measured by a number of factors. A community is a
group of people whose connections and relations are formed
by their shared history, traditions, experiences, geographies
and identities. Let's look at two high-profile cases: the writer
Joseph Boyden and the director Michelle Latimer, the latter
of whom doubled down on her suspect claims in an interview
with the *Globe and Mail* earlier this month. Neither of them can
establish anything beyond the most tenuous of DNA links, and
neither of them can establish substantive identifiers of belonging to the Indigenous community. Regardless of the outcome of
spitting in a test tube, those banking on DNA to demonstrate
their Indigeneity simply cannot be considered Indigenous.
There is no way of telling precisely when or how a drop of
Indigenous blood ended up in a settler's DNA, and it most
certainly does not confirm membership in any particular

group. How would a person have established themselves as Indigenous pre-DNA testing? By way of what has always been done: identifying connections through shared history, community, tradition, geography and family.

I often think of Mr Boyden's insistent claim articulated in the form of a meme: him proudly crossing his arms so we can see his feather tattoos, sporting a Chicago Blackhawks T-shirt, completely tone-deaf to the decades-long struggle to end the era of Indigenous peoples being reduced to sports-team logos and mascots. He states, almost petulantly: "If I have been traditionally adopted by a number of people in Indigenous communities, if my DNA test shows I have Indigenous blood, if I have engaged my whole career defending Indigenous rights, am I not, in some way, Indigenous?"

No, Mr Boyden. You absolutely are not. Even if he were adopted by an entire community, as opposed to a few individuals making space for him, that would not make him Indigenous. It would make him adopted. Just as an adopted child can never be made the biological child of the adoptive parents, a person adopted by an Indigenous community becomes welcomed and accepted as a part of the community but is not magically, suddenly, Indigenous. Mr Boyden claims to have defended Indigenous rights his whole career and that this advocacy should privilege him with the right to call himself Indigenous. Should every non-Indigenous lawyer who has fought in solidarity with Indigenous peoples for the recognition of our rights be considered Indigenous? The very idea is preposterous.

As for the Indigenous individuals and/or communities that have or will elect to adopt Play Indians, it is their right to do so. That is their own business, which must be respected, just as it must be respected that such adoption does not render the adoptee Indigenous.

The residential school legacy and many other limitations and imperatives imposed on Indigenous peoples were and are entrenched in the law. Virtually every aspect of Indigenous life has been legislated and controlled by policy arising from law. For white settler descendants, this kind of domestic or settler hegemony goes hand in hand with a perceived birthright to everything. The history of this country is based on the taking of everything from Indigenous people. It is not controversial that Canada's colonial period (and post-colonial period) was and is nothing less than brutal for Indigenous people. Neither is it controversial that the deep harms done to Indigenous peoples during colonial times remain and are often exacerbated by the systemic nature in which Canada continues to reflect its colonial foundation.

This is where Play Indians find such a deeply ingrained sense of entitlement. They believe it is within their right, should they so deign, to usurp our very being and make it over in their own noble savage image. This is not a new phenomenon. The work of Dr Darryl Leroux of Saint Mary's University follows the emergence of the so-called Eastern Métis, and further identifies and analyzes a long history of pretendianism dating back to the 1600s. The term *aspirational descent* evolved from the academic works of Dr Leroux and Dr Kim TallBear, among others, and refers to those Caucasians who assert a claim to Indigeneity even when it is roundly found to be false. These charlatans aspire to an identity they believe will give them an advantage or benefit of some sort, even if that benefit is a proud sense of self they can't find in their true identity.

Many Indigenous people who lost touch with their ancestry through colonial efforts at assimilation and termination suffer great loss and struggle through their lifetimes looking to reconnect with family, territory and tradition. In the face of this, it is exponentially egregious when individuals, already occupying a position of privilege, use that privilege to assume an imagined persona as an Indigenous person. At a certain crossroads, these Play Indians determine that their lives will be improved if they pretend they are something they are not.

To all you Play Indians, if you want to play Indian in your own back yard, like the children I watched decades ago, well, it's your yard. Playing the noble savage there will not harm too many people, but playing it out in the world, our world, most certainly does. Pretendianism is no different than the Indian Agent telling the Indians just exactly how they are to be, stripping away the reality of being Indigenous in Canada which, in addition to the beauty of who we are, is characterized by the highest likelihood for poverty, violent death, suicide, incarceration, homelessness and addiction. It's easier to embrace us when you don't have to worry about being among the almost 100 percent of Indigenous women who are sexually assaulted; or that you live on a reserve with no potable water; or that you or your relative may be incarcerated because you or he couldn't afford a lawyer and stood no chance in a system riddled with systemic racism; or your relative (like mine) might be dead because he was the wrong colour looking for help on a country road. These terrible assaults on Indigenous people are among the shared experiences we have that form our bonds of community and have done so for more than 500 years. These Play Indians have neither the intergenerational knowledge that binds our people together as community nor the intergenerational trauma—the scars of colonialism we uniquely bear, recognizable only to one another. As I once wrote in a poem, "we know our own relations by our star quilts made of ghosts."

And then, of course, there is the inauthentic and uninformed manner in which Play Indians represent what it means to be Indigenous. In effect, they alter Indigenous reality by representing their sanitized and contrived ideas as real, wielding their privilege to render genuinely Indigenous people powerless to object or, importantly, to correct.

Further, the phenomenon adds layers of complexity for Indigenous people trying to find their way home. As more and more Play Indians are exposed, some Indigenous individuals and communities are becoming wary of people who very well might be legitimately Indigenous. So many of our communities are generous and welcoming to people coming home. Yet it is deeply embarrassing to be duped by play actors pulling the wool over our eyes. Not wanting to be burned twice (or a hundred times), I see Indigenous people becoming more reticent about accepting self-identification. My beautiful, gentle Nokom would have welcomed any person into her home, made them tea and fed them. Maybe she wouldn't have been so welcoming if she were being lied to with some regularity. So it goes with our communities in response to Play Indians. Their fakery becomes a change agent in the Indigenous community, as open arms are replaced by increased suspicion.

Recently, following the outing of Michelle Latimer, Haida filmmaker Tamara Bell came forward promoting the idea of legislation similar to the American Indian Arts and Crafts Act. This Act acknowledges the unique ownership of Indigenous art, and levies hefty fines—up to $250,000—and jail terms of up to five years as penalties for non-Indigenous artisans who fraudulently present their art as Indigenous. She notes correctly that Canada tends to turn a blind eye to this kind of fraudulent profiteering. I would add that Canada takes, at best, a *tsk-tsk* approach. Or worse, literary and other luminaries defend the Play Indians as though it is Indigenous people who are misguided in their efforts to protect a place in the literary, art and academic worlds—places we did not enter easily or without struggle. Notably, the American Act does not apply to literary works or film productions.

I do believe that, given these insidious, pervasive and ongoing actions by non-Indigenous writers and filmmakers, the time is right for comparable legislation in Canada. Such an Act would be quite different in this country, given our legislative tradition of proportionality, and it would require inclusion of literary and film works in its definition of art. Certainly, when a lucrative career can be forged on a false identity, and the Play Indians remain undaunted by moral outrage, there must be recourse in the law.

Every time another Play Indian is exposed, I feel as though someone has pulled the rug from under me, incredulous that it's still happening. We can't go back in time and gently correct those kids with their plastic tomahawks. They are grandparents now. What have their children and grandchildren absorbed from those beliefs entrenched on the playground? Colonial attitudes of oppression are intergenerational. We are equally powerless to erase the discomfort and confusion of little Indigenous kids watching such games and how they add to the colonial browbeating that's a central feature in Indigenous lives. But if we talk the talk of supporting the rights of Indigenous peoples, surely that must start with standing firm against fakery. No matter the quality of the art produced by these Play Indians, they must be held accountable for using their privilege to step over the backs of Indigenous people to reach for their golden ticket.

THE SUN IS ALWAYS IN YOUR EYES IN REXDALE

Kunal Chaudhary

On a perfectly idyllic afternoon in Rexdale 15 years ago, my brother and I stood in blue school uniforms on a street lined with scrawny trees and pale brick houses. A car idled on the road beside us. One skinny hand stuck out the window and pointed the silver barrel of a gun in our direction. The man holding the gun smiled, caught in a laugh. "What do you think about this?" he shouted. My brother pivoted his body in front of mine. We grimaced. This was the end we had been expecting.

At home, our parents interpreted the scene the only way they knew how. "What were they?" my father asked. My brother looked at him uncomprehendingly. "Were they brown? Black?" We knew the answer he expected, but the truth is that, in Rexdale, the sun is in your eyes all the time. We couldn't remember. My brother hastened a guess. "West Indian?" It was not good enough. My father called it a "freak incident," and we never spoke of it again.

These Are Not the Stories I Tell

Years later, when I tell people I grew up in Rexdale, this is the kind of story they seem to want to hear. "How bad was it?"

they'll ask. Sometimes, I tell them about the time I almost got smoked on my way home from school. Other times, I allude to the fights, the first time I felt my fist press into flesh. These have all the elements of a good anecdote: tension, violence, catharsis.

They do not want to hear about our life growing up in a basement on Upper Humber Drive, in a house with a vegetable garden and an apple tree and the sounds of Highway 427 muffled behind a massive concrete divider at the end of our backyard. They do not want to hear about the subsidized swimming lessons at the Humber Community Pool, or the Sikh man who sold mangoes out of a van on the shoulder of Humberline Drive. Nor do they want to know about "Dr Flea," the elusive, Gatsby-like figure who ran the largest flea market in the city a short distance from our home, a place where we spent hours browsing bargain-bin clothes and video games before pooling all our cash for necessities. These are not the stories I tell.

My family immigrated to Canada and settled in Rexdale in 2002, shortly after 9/11 made the tint of our skin a liability in this country. Seeing the neatly-clipped lawns and uniform houses of Upper Humber Drive, my brother thought we had walked onto the set of *Small Wonder*. "This is heaven," he said the first time we drove into the neighbourhood. My parents had asked their friends in Brampton for a home in the heart of the city. This was it.

For the first few years of our life in this country, we lived in crushing anonymity. In the gaze of early-aughts daily news and cable television, we did not exist. So we spent a lot of time moulding our voices, our clothes, and our mannerisms to mimic the whiteness we saw on screen. Even in a school where you could count the number of white kids on the fingers of one hand, whiteness was the norm. So we tried to adapt. We ate Black Diamond cheese with Wonder Bread, performed Christmas and Easter with cheap, imported traditions. In the absence of representation, we lived parodies of white lives.

In postcards, Toronto is the 15 square kilometres around the CN Tower—a needle next to a dome crouched among skyscrapers. This Toronto sits at the centre of the Canadian national imaginary. To this day, I find it impossible to consolidate that image of the glittering city with the obscurity in which I grew up. Rexdale stood at the centre of nothing.

The Year of the Gun

All this changed in 2005. The number of gun-related deaths in the city doubled from the previous year as 52 people lost their lives. Five of these shootings happened in Rexdale. Media coverage of the gun violence in Toronto's inner suburbs ramped up dramatically, often converging on racialized, low-income communities such as Rexdale, Jane and Finch, and Malvern. In our basement apartment, where TV news blared constantly, we stopped to listen every time "Rexdale" was mentioned on screen. The media dubbed it "the year of the gun."

The previous year, a landmark study, *Poverty by Postal Code*, mapped the drift in concentrated poverty in Toronto from mixed-income communities downtown out to strictly working-class neighbourhoods in the suburbs of Etobicoke, North York, and Scarborough. The analysis spanned 20-odd years and found that there had been a "profound shift in the resident profile of higher poverty neighbourhoods, with 'poor' visible minority immigrant families making up far larger percentages of the total 'poor' family population in these neighbourhoods." To combat the significant gaps in public infrastructure and services available to families living in places such as Rexdale, the study recommended a slew of material interventions including affordable housing, wage subsidies, employment programs, and the revitalization of public spaces.

Unfortunately, by August 2005, when the *Toronto Star* printed 33 guns on its front page, one for each shooting-related death in the city, under the headline, "The Other Toronto," the problem of Toronto's poor, racialized inner suburbs had become indistinguishable from the anxious conversation surrounding guns and gang violence in the city. In other words, guns became the only story about our neighbourhood that mattered.

Amy Siciliano, then a PhD student at the University of Toronto, wrote her dissertation on the impact of the "year of the gun" on Toronto's racialized poor. She spoke to policy-makers, police, public-housing experts, health workers, and a broad selection of invested community members.

"Absent from popular discourse and official policy documents was the crucial fact that the sharp spike in gun violence was not a result of increasing concentrations of racialized poverty in the inner suburbs," she wrote in *Policing Poverty: Race, Space and the Fear of Crime after the Year of the Gun*. Instead, she discovered it was actually the result of a massive gang raid conducted by Toronto police in 2004 that busted up the "Malvern Crew"—an alleged gang operation out of Scarborough. This raid, conducted under the banner "Project Impact," led to 500 criminal charges and the arrest of 15 gang elders. It was the largest gang raid conducted in the city at the time.

Siciliano wrote that this raid specifically—and not the abstract evil of concentrated racialized poverty—set off the spike in shootings in 2005. As one of her research participants put it: "they busted up a bunch of these gangs and sent all of the gang elders to the clang and so there were a lot of 15- and 16-year-olds without elders who didn't . . . understand that you're not supposed to shoot up your neighbourhood, and so it was mayhem."

Instead of addressing the threat that aggressive policing posed to Black and brown communities, then-mayor David Miller responded to the violence of the summer of 2005 with a plan for targeted investment in 13 new "priority neighbourhoods"—including Jamestown, in Rexdale. Meanwhile, the provincial government hired an additional 26 officers and 32 attorneys for its "guns and gangs task force."

The perceived crisis of gun violence and the racialized communities it stemmed from came to a head on Boxing Day, 2005. Jane Creba, a white teenager out shopping near the Eaton Centre, was caught in the crossfire of a gang-related shooting and killed. According to Siciliano, this was when gun violence "penetrated the [overwhelmingly white and middle-class] social space of the urban core." Despite the deaths of dozens of Black men that year as a result of gun violence, Creba's death was declared the moment that Toronto lost its innocence. Days later, the provincial government earmarked an additional $51 million in the fight against gun crime in the GTA.

This was how gun violence in Toronto's racialized inner suburbs ceased to be understood as a side-effect of sledgehammer policing and material deprivation and became, instead, a root-malignancy that only the police could excise. The criminalization of our communities was complete.

"Guns and Gangs"

It did not matter that only one area within Rexdale had been designated as a priority neighbourhood. In the words of *Toronto Star* columnist Christopher Hume, Rexdale as a whole had become "shorthand for suburban blight, social breakdown, and gang violence."

In school, the unctuous rhetoric of "guns and gangs" seeped down from our provincial legislature, through cracks in the media and education system, and rained down on our heads. Teachers gathered us together and led hushed discussions about gang violence, ubiquitously defining gangs for us as "a group of four or more people loitering without a purpose." This definition was repeated to us in almost every conversation we had about gun violence. The administration held trade-in drives where we exchanged toy guns and gun-shaped toys for less alarming playthings—an experience not shared by friends who grew up white and middle-class. We were required to purchase mesh gym bags with the implicit (but universally understood) purpose of making it impossible to conceal a firearm. Explicitly and repeatedly, we were told not to wear "coloured bandanas or do-rags that might signal gang affiliation."

I attended a school called Humberwood Downs that was part of a huge money pit on the edge of Rexdale known as the Humberwood Centre. This was a wide low-rise complex with a roof that looked like a set of raised eyebrows. It had been developed as a joint $23 million investment in a community with little access to public amenities outside its walls. The Centre housed two schools, a public library, a community centre, and a daycare. For the most part, the investment paid off in spades. The complex was an oasis in a resource desert. Humberwood Downs would eventually be described in the *National Post* as a school "as close to private as any in the Toronto District School Board."

By the time the "year of the gun" rolled around, however, many of the students in Humberwood had already experienced the sensation of being viewed as essentially—or at least potentially—criminal. For years, our teachers and administrators informed us that the school had a "zero-tolerance policy" for "play-fighting." This policy was enforced through innumerable detentions, suspensions, and exhortations that "play-fighting is real fighting." The nebulousness of this definition made it so that anything from punching your friend in the arm to tackling someone during a game of tag could be grounds for punishment. For the child (almost always a boy) who failed to keep his hands to himself, the institutional response to "play-fighting" would be his first experience of criminalization.

Zero tolerance for "bad behaviour" in Ontario schools had been codified into the *Education Act* in 2000 by the Tory education minister Janet Ecker under an amendment called the *Safe Schools Act*. Starting in September 2001, the new law gave teachers the power to directly suspend students and sketched out a poorly-defined set of checks and balances in which such a move was appropriate. Most dramatically, according to the Ontario Human Rights Commission, the Act also provisioned "mandatory suspension and expulsion and police involvement . . . for a wide range of infractions." Months before I moved to Rexdale, Ecker had introduced the language of policing into our schools and deployed the police as muscle in the retributive punishment of children.

Consider fighting: in the TDSB, fighting was grounds for mandatory suspension. If, as our teachers said, "play-fighting was real fighting," then simple rough-and-tumble play was framed as pathological and criminal. When we did get into "serious" fights, the threat of zero-tolerance made it impossible for us to explore the frustrations and antagonisms that provoked them.

I got into my first real fight in 2004, with a boy named Navdeep. We had been messing with each other for weeks, and things came to a head one afternoon on the playground. He got me on the ground and struck me blindly a few times. I rolled him over and cracked my fist into his jaw. The second I did it, it turned my stomach. A rush of complex emotions— guilt, shock, horror—flooded my system. We caught sight of a teacher in our periphery and stopped immediately, sitting on the grass and pantomiming friendship till his gaze turned away. I remember recognizing, in the moment, that I was far more terrified of my teacher than I was of the boy throwing his fists at me. Fighting meant anything from detention to having the police called on you. Navdeep knew this too. So we sat there, nervously, and performed the absence of pain. We policed our bodies before they could be policed for us.

Eventually, Dalton McGuinty's Liberal government overturned the *Safe Schools Act*. They replaced it with the *Progressive Discipline and School Safety Act* in 2007, primarily because of a complaint by the Ontario Human Rights Commission that demonstrated the disproportionate impact Ecker's hard-line legislation had on racialized, especially Black, students.

In 2005, however, the "year of the gun" exacerbated the criminalizing effect of the *Safe Schools Act*. As the constant barrage of noise about gun violence permeated our lives from the news, our parents and our teachers, it became clear to us as children that the adults we looked up to saw us as the source of all this troubling violence. The well-intentioned toy-gun drives, school assemblies, and extended conversations about signalling gang affiliation tinged the generous programming at Humberwood with paternalism and surveillance. Slowly, we grew aware that the pottery studio, the full industrial kitchen, the two libraries, the artist residencies, and the heavily-sub-sidized extracurricular programming were not there to lift our spirits and cultivate our minds but rather to contain our inherent destructiveness. Being children, we came to see our-selves this way too: as nuisances, burdens, scourges of the very society we had been struggling to assimilate into for years.

Our lives resisted this mythology of violence, of course. After school, the public library at the Humberwood Centre would be crowded with students elbowing each other for a spot on the computer. Others lounged about reading books by R L Stine and Roald Dahl. In our blue Humberwood uni-forms, we often jokingly play-acted Bloods and Crips with the maroon-clad students of Holy Child, the neighbouring Cath-olic school, before slumping to the foot of the bookshelves in the adult section to read in the hour before our parents picked us up. Our teachers put on galleries to celebrate our artwork and threw assemblies for all the holidays we celebrated that were never designated as days off. They did have a talent for identifying the best in each child and nurturing it. Unfortu-nately, the perceived ubiquity of violence in our community muted the best of their efforts. It kept us scared, defensive, and distrustful of almost everyone around us.

If we felt this as South Asian children, the impact was only more pronounced on Rexdale's Black children. At the time, my neighbourhood in Rexdale was 40 percent South Asian and 17 percent Black. As media saturation and systemic discrimination equated Blackness with chaotic and unpredictable violence, we were conditioned to draw a line between ourselves and our Black classmates. Of course, we were doing this long before Janet Ecker and Jane Creba. A virulent strain of anti-Blackness has existed in South Asian communities since time immemorial. We were the aggressors too.

Casual Colourism

Not long after we moved to our basement apartment on Upper Humber Drive, my mother began throwing great, profligate dinner parties for the network of Indian families that we had befriended in the community. In the absence of accessible public spaces, many immigrants in Rexdale turned their homes into ad-hoc community centres, privacy giving way to communion and commiseration. Imagine Trinity Bellwoods on a Saturday, but crammed into 700 windowless square feet.

As the darker of two brothers, I was often pulled aside by my aunties as they gossiped aloud about my complexion. They wondered if I would grow to lighten, and stood me beside my light-skinned brother to gawk. This sort of casual colourism is common in many South Asian households. Imported from the old country, it often blends seamlessly into the ambient anti-Blackness in this one. As children, we oscillated between the prejudices imposed by our parents and a more fundamental desire to engage with our Black classmates.

Here's a story: in 2006, I made a friend named Imran. He was from Egypt and had shuttled around a handful of schools by the time I met him. Imran was the only other kid in my class who snuck novels into the folds of his textbooks and devoured them during math lessons. We became fast friends.

He was whip-smart and boisterous, and had a habit of pulling me into a headlock when we walked together. For months, I would go home and regale my parents with stories about our playground adventures, the frenetic conversations we had that spanned all of recess and spilled into lunch.

A couple of months into this friendship, my parents met Imran at the Humber Community Pool. We tumbled in the water, dunked our heads below the surface and competed to see who could hold their breath the longest. Imran had a brown name and a Black body. He was just out of earshot when my parents pulled me aside and told me I should be more careful about my choice in friends.

I remember the way their warning cast a pall over our friendship. I began to see his boisterousness, his hyperactivity, with suspicion. Were these the signs of inevitable criminality? Was he one of the "bad influences" we were warned about? Most frighteningly: would he draw me in, make me a "bad kid" too? We grew distant. A few months later, he left and I never saw him again.

In the process of researching this article, I reminded my parents about Imran. They were mortified. "I'm ready to say *mea culpa*," my dad said. "We were just so scared for you. I don't know why we were scared." Old friends I spoke to recall the way everyone punctuated insults with the N-word, the way we scapegoated our Black classmates at the first sign of trouble. We're all mortified too.

Being From "That Place"

I left Rexdale in 2007, a few months after a teenager named Jordan Manners was shot and killed in a stairwell at C. W. Jefferys Collegiate Institute near Keele and Finch. We moved to Parkwoods, a similarly troubled but mercifully ignored corner of North York, on the edge of Scarborough.

It was on my first day of school in Parkwoods that I realized none of what I had experienced in Rexdale was "normal." In Parkwoods, there were no more toy-gun drives, no more administrators fussing over colours, no more presumptions of inherent violence. Nobody felt the need to perform civility for our teachers.

As a matter of chance, one of my Black classmates from Humberwood had moved to the area at the same time our family did. I saw him during lunch, dressed in clothes I didn't recognize, smiling in conversation with a kid I didn't know. I was thrilled to see a familiar face, but when I went up to him to say hello, he dragged me aside by the arm and his expression turned grave. He told me he didn't want people knowing he was from "that place."

"We don't know each other, okay?"

After the death of Jordan Manners, Premier Dalton McGuinty commissioned a task force to investigate the causes of youth violence and to "find out what might be done to address them to make Ontario safer in the long term."

This task force eventually published a report called the *Roots of Youth Violence* that lucidly articulated the risk factors for violent crime. These included poverty, racism, poor community design, and criminalization through the education system.

"Poverty does not directly cause violent crime," the report read, "but poverty without hope, poverty with isolation, poverty with hunger and poor living conditions, poverty with racism and poverty with numerous daily reminders of social exclusion can lead to the immediate risk factors for violence."

It's simple, the report seemed to say: the solution to violent crime has always been the alleviation of poverty and social isolation. The trouble with this narrative is its very simplicity. There is real discursive comfort in framing conversations about material deprivation around gun violence.

In 2006, when all those shootings went down, the *Globe and Mail* patted Toronto police on the back for a job well done. Meanwhile, housing affordability continued to decline and the economic disparities between Toronto's racialized inner suburbs and the downtown core continued to grow. The legacy media outlets that dictate the state of discourse in this city persisted with their grim fixation on gun violence while broadly neglecting the remainder of our lives. *The Safe Schools Act* was disbanded, but the Board of Education introduced police officers directly into "high-risk" schools in the city, including my high school. We were still expected to live invisibly, or as objects of suspicion worthy of surveillance.

And over the next decade, gun violence rose steadily too.

In 2018, the number of gun deaths in Toronto spiked again, and another "year of the gun" was enshrined into our collective history. Millions were poured into further policing. That year, I began my first job out of college as a teacher. Waiting for the subway, I would see "Rexdale" flash on the news feed on the station video monitors, always in relation to another gun death, another shooting. Two years later, I would see Rexdale on the news again, soaked red on a map comparing infection rates of Covid-19 in the city—another institutional failure pinned on the people with whom I grew up, and whom I would watch fall ill one by one as the pandemic spread.

We are still waiting on a better story.

WHY THE FILET-O-FISH
IS MY GOLD STANDARD
FOR FAST FOOD

Jane Hu

One of the first Chinese McDonald's opened on April 23, 1992, in Beijing, the largest in the world, at the time. I never got to eat there: My mother was busy packing our things. Two weeks after it opened, she and I were on a plane bound for Montreal to join my father, who was then completing a postdoc that would leave him broke for years. What I remember most from that period was how little we did. My mother worked weekend shifts at a sock factory, while my father took over at home. He studied in our one-bedroom apartment, and I watched TV. On special occasions, we went to McDonald's.

In Canada, just like in China, eating at McDonald's was a novelty for us. In the wake of post-Mao economic reforms, the belated introduction of the Golden Arches to China represented a whole ethos about what constituted the good life. Fast food might connote easy accessibility or overindulgence in the West, but McDonald's presented a different kind of comfort for my family and me. The cost of a burger was hardly a trivial thing for us at the time, and my parents didn't actually treat me to meals there all that often. When they did, we always got takeout so we could eat our burgers and fries around our

Formica dining table, on our own plates. The hope was to have our fast food as slowly as we could.

The Filet-O-Fish became my menu item of choice. Its virtues are too many to count; doing so would be futile. As McDonald's' only seafood-based option, the Filet-O-Fish's semblance of relative health appealed to my parents. Luckily it was also McDonald's' most delicious item. It played to my Chinese palate: While other McDonald's buns were toasted, the Filet-O-Fish's was steamed, much like the baozi. From its honeyed starch to its tangy tartar and savory filet, the taste of the Filet-O-Fish carries an ineffable umami-ness. At once sweet and sour, it reminds me of orange-chicken sauce: a plausibly Chinese flavor mass-produced in America. Eating one always felt transportive—the equivalent of Proust's madeleine for my Chinese diasporic upbringing.

The Filet-O-Fish is the gold standard of fast food for many Asian-Americans, as well as other minority American communities. Invented by an Ohio franchise owner in 1962, the first Filet-O-Fish was the answer to the problem of McDonald's' falling sales on Fridays, when observant Catholics abstained from eating meat. Born from an attempt to market fast food to as many people as possible, the tasty little unit has since been further claimed by everyone from fish-loving Chinese-Americans to practicing Muslims to—well, anyone with taste. By 1965 the sandwich had gone national.

Its appeal is inscrutable, perhaps out of proportion to its paltry constituent parts. Consider the recognizably flaky fish patty, made from the ubiquitous Alaskan pollock. "Pollock is everywhere," writes the marine fisheries biologist Kevin M Bailey in the book *Billion-Dollar Fish*. "It is the pure white meat in fish sticks bought at Walmart and Filet-O-Fish burgers ordered in McDonald's." But you wouldn't want the fish to be more interesting. The generic quality of pollock's fishiness—common enough for various cuisines to lay claim to it—is part of its allure. So maybe what makes the sandwich beloved isn't its taste at all, but the juxtaposition of its elements: A single filet of fried fish, topped with a thin slice of American cheese and tartar sauce, all of it cradled in a bun whose impossible roundness suggests the triumph of industrial food production.

As a child, I was under the fantasy that my obsession with such a strange sandwich was eccentric. When I went to McDonald's with friends who got Chicken McNuggets Happy Meals or cheeseburgers, ordering the Filet-O-Fish made me feel as if I was in on some sort of secret. After a few years in Montreal, my dad landed a good government job in Victoria, British Columbia. On our drive across Canada, we indulged in the prospect of my dad's earning a real salary by eating at McDonald's almost daily, a whirlwind of Filet-O-Fish meals (for me) and hamburgers (for my parents). But my experience was shattered when I, fancying myself different, pointed out that my parents both loved hamburgers while I, a renegade, preferred the Filet-O-Fish. "Well, I like the Filet-O-Fish most too," my mother put it candidly. "But it is expensive, so we only buy it for you."

These days, the sandwich is more expensive than ever; it's also less beautiful than I remember. At some point, the Filet-O-Fish underwent rebranding: An ostentatious paper box replaced the modest blue wrapper, while what I remember being a full slice of cheese seems to have shrunk by half. McDonald's insists that the cheese has always been half a slice—so as not to overwhelm the fishiness of the fillet. Today's unboxing experience most often reveals limp cheese sagging off the patty, frequently stuck to the ill-advised box. Where is the madeleine of my youth? Nowadays, a good Filet-O-Fish is hard to find.

And yet, I eat the thing. I look for the Filet-O-Fish on every drunken late-night McDonald's run, rushing to order two of them 10 minutes before closing. Yes, my adulthood has been marked by disappointments, but ultimately I take what I can get. The Filet-O-Fish remains my platonic ideal of fast food, however imperfect it has become. And perhaps its imperfections, the way it never quite lives up to the ideal, are what make the sandwich feel like home.

QUITTING AMERICA

ME Rogan

I'm seven years old, and under my bed is a go bag for when I head over the wall. Inside the green plastic garbage bag are a few stuffed animals that I take out every night and return each morning. A fraying rabbit, Winnie-the-Pooh, a Rin Tin Tin dog. It's not always the same three that make it into the go bag. I line up all my stuffed animals and decide which I can take with me. My older sister watches but never says a word. She knows there is no way out, but I still see potential openings. Our tall bedroom window looks out onto the back porch and has a wooden screen that can be removed only from the outside. When no one is watching, I sneak around to the porch and loosen as many swivel clips as I can reach. At the grocery store, I wander off from my mother and six older siblings and try to look like a child who needs rescuing, like I wouldn't make a sound if someone snatched me away.

Nobody takes the bait. It will be fifty years before I make it over the wall on my own.

It was 1968 and I was stranded deep in the wilds of New York's Westchester County with my parents, five brothers, sister, and 250 boys who had been sent to Lincoln Hall by the state to be rehabilitated for their petty crimes and truancy.

Lincoln Hall was well camouflaged. Its expansive property was bisected by Route 202, a highway bounded by old stone walls that meandered through the southern tip of New York state and across the Hudson River. The Lincoln Hall campus encompassed a new chapel, a gymnasium with gleaming hardwood, an outdoor quarter-mile running track, a manicured baseball diamond, a swimming pool, handball courts, and a movie theatre. The entire property, on both sides of Route 202, was surrounded by acres of farmland.

Lincoln Hall was run by the De La Salle Christian Brothers with a handful of lay staff. Our family of nine had moved out of the Bronx two years earlier. Our parents, Ed and Pat, sold the brothers on a package deal—my mother, Pat, would be the school's librarian, and Ed the new assistant vice-principal. Neither had the formal requirements for their jobs. Pat told anyone who asked that she was inspired by the Hollywood blockbuster *Boys Town*, starring Spencer Tracy as the real-life Father Flanagan. Ed looked the part of a man who could keep troubled youth in line, with his regulation Navy crewcut and the American bald eagle on his forearm. When we first arrived, Ed called Lincoln Hall a "country club for delinquents." His office was on the main floor of the Fishbowl, an L-shaped red-brick building with wide glass double-doors framed by a semicircular portico. Near Ed's office were the locked cells for the boys who acted up or tried to run away. When a Linky kid jumped the wall, it was Ed's job to fetch him back and drop him in the cells for a few days.

Pat had negotiated our housing on Lincoln Hall property as part of the package deal. We lived on the ground floor of what was then the Lakeview, a 100-year-old house without lake or view. Ed sunk a pole into the front lawn and raised the American flag every morning. Every night, he picked two of his children to lower the flag and fold it into tight military triangles. On Sunday nights, Ed ironed his five white work shirts, then polished both his pairs of black penny loafers and both his pairs of brown penny loafers, in that order.

Life at the Lakeview was a roulette of transgressions. It always started the same way. Ed and Pat lined the seven of us up in the kitchen in age order. Ed promised nobody would get hit if we told him the truth. He wanted to know who broke into the locked fridge, who stuck gum on the dog, who left the car window open, who ate his pistachios, moved one of his razor blades, busted the couch, put a hole in the screen door, or drank the Vicks cough syrup. Sometimes there was no transgression at all.

Ed began at one end of the line and worked his way down to me. "Was it you?" Each *No* bought you a crack across the side of your head, clipping your ear with his Knights of Columbus ring. My oldest brother's hands would fly up to cover his inflamed face, a scalded combination of fear and confusion. When my brother cried, Ed sneered, "Why are you crying? Tell me why you're crying."

Ed was a lefty but swung right with my second oldest brother, the only redhead in the lot, born with a misshapen ear and a birthmark on the side of his head. The ear was off limits. That was Pat's rule. Pat liked to tell the story that she had seen her husband cry only twice: the first time he saw his son's birthmark and when JFK was assassinated. Down the line, my brother with the bullet-shaped head, the beefiest of all the boys, would jut his jaw out to enrage Ed even more. It always worked.

Once, the middle brother, with sanguine hazel eyes the size of half dollars, jumped the gun and confessed just to get it all over with. It didn't work. "You think I'm a fool?" My sister stared at the ground, shoulders rounded, plucking at the ends of her too-short shirt sleeves and hiccupping from fear and tears. "I bet you feel sorry for yourself." I could feel our collective rage gather and dissolve with each pass up and down the line.

Ed talked a lot when he beat his kids. He liked to lean in close, looking at your forehead instead of your eyes. With spittle at the corners of his mouth, he would remind you that you had no problems. "You think you have problems? You don't know what a problem is. I've got real problems. You've got it made."

After making his way up and down the line a few times with no result, Ed would turn to Pat and begin their canned exchange. What followed was part Beckett, part vaudeville.

"How did this happen to us, Pat? How did we get saddled with seven lying sacks of shit?" Pat would sigh and cock her head to one side, resigned, heartbroken. "To have to raise savages. A pack of animals: Thieves. Did we miss something? The roof over their heads, the food on their plates—Isn't it enough?"

When they'd run through their script, Ed would pull out the big guns. It was the final, violent punctuation of the battering. Vile slurs we knew were wrong—vile even for the time we lived in. "I go to work every day and have to deal with ni**ers and s**cs. Do you think I want to work with those animals? Do you think your mother wants to work with ni**ers and s**cs and then come home to this? You kids? Seven lying sacks of shit?"

Ed and Pat would take a well-timed smoke break so we could spin a butter knife on the kitchen table to choose a victim. We watched the beating that came next. Afterward, with scarlet faces and ears ringing, we were piled into the car for King Kone ice cream, careful not to drop a sprinkle on Ed's car seats.

If Ed was methodical in his violence, Pat was chaotic, hijacked by despair. She brandished a shotgun at her children. She grabbed knives from the kitchen and accused us of wanting her dead. She tore through the house at odd hours, cursing the man who had stuffed her full of babies and ruined her life. She would leave the house in her nightgown with an empty suitcase to sit at the end of the long gravel driveway, waiting for one of the boys to coax her back inside. Ed always played possum, asleep in his La-Z-Boy, until she spun herself out.

We were told, "What happens in this house stays in this house." They needn't have worried. At six, I stopped speaking for a while. I couldn't drag a single word out of my mouth. I was terrified Ed and Pat were going to hell. I prayed for my parents and did my best to sound sincere. I worried that I couldn't be a good person in a family like this and that maybe we'd all go to hell together. At St. Joseph Elementary School, we stood with our hands over our hearts, facing the American flag, and recited the Pledge of Allegiance every morning. The nuns told us how to be good: carry orange UNICEF boxes at Halloween, pray for African babies, keep our hands and feet to ourselves, keep our mouths zipped in the hallways, and most of all, never lie.

The first lie I ever told myself was that I couldn't run away from home because I loved my family. I told myself that my brothers and sister would never survive without me, that I mattered to them. I ran sentences in my head, practised lies to defend against the futility of my useless go bag. I told myself that I loved my father, and that I loved my mother, even when they beat me.

I did love my family, but that wasn't why I stayed. A seven-year-old has nowhere to go.

On October 25, 2018, after more than three decades living and working in Canada, I walked into the American embassy in Ottawa and renounced my American citizenship. As instructed by my lawyer and embassy officials, I carried only a slim valise. Inside were a fistful of US government forms, my American passport for surrender, my American birth certificate, my Social Security card, and my Canadian passport to prove I would not be stateless after my renunciation. The valise also held a self-addressed Express-Post envelope, to receive my Certificate of Loss of Nationality once the US State Department had stamped its final approval, and a cashier's cheque for $2,350 (US)—my exit fee.

My formal renunciation was the final step in a byzantine two-year journey that began when I applied to become a

Canadian citizen a few months before the 2016 US presidential election. My creeping fear had evolved into grim certainty that Donald Trump would win. I was desperate to shed all birthright ties to my country.

Until the 2016 election, I'd always thought of my childhood as an outlier, so extreme that I couldn't shoehorn it into a larger narrative. It wasn't until Trump's transgressive campaign—the ominous stalking of Hillary Clinton on a debate stage, the grotesque pantomime of a disabled reporter and fusillade of racist statements at his rallies—that I recognized my family as a diorama of America's dysfunction. As I watched Trump lie in real time, disavowing reality while inciting violence, I realized that my family shared the same superpower: we could hide in plain sight, lie to ourselves, and make others believe it. And, just as Trump would disproportionately attack anyone who threatened to unmask him, we would go to any lengths to protect our lies.

Once, I walked into the kitchen just as Pat whipped her Bloody Mary at Ed's head. She missed, and the tumbler exploded against the wall behind him. I was certain she had shot him. One of my brothers tried to comfort me and said this kind of thing happened in all families. I knew that wasn't true. When Ed and Pat stopped eating meals with us and instead brought their plates of better food and pitchers of cold Tom Collins into the living room each night, I knew that that wasn't normal either.

When Ed and Pat trotted us out in public, people would marvel at their outsize brood and how well behaved we were, how scrubbed clean we looked in Pat's handmade clothing. They couldn't hear Ed's *sotto voce* in our ears, his breath on the backs of our necks as he'd lean over with a smile on his face if anyone was acting up and warn, "Fuck with me now and you're fucking with your heartbeat," or, "I'm going to lose my shoe up your ass when we get home," or, "I'm going to knock you into the middle of next week."

At home, my family was a cauldron of threats and violence. Outside of the Lakeview, America was seething. Early in 1968, South Carolina Highway Patrol officers fired into a crowd of student protesters at South Carolina State University, a historically Black school in Orangeburg. Three Black students were shot dead. In April of that year, Martin Luther King Jr.'s assassination ignited widespread rioting that escalated into shoot-to-kill orders. Antiwar demonstrations on college campuses spread across the country even as the US increased troop deployment in Vietnam. The Democratic National Convention in Chicago turned into a televised brawl. Richard Nixon ran on a "law and order" campaign that won him the 1968 presidential election, then dog-whistled about the rise of Afro-centrism and the Black Panther Party.

In 1972, right before his second term, Nixon's White House was under investigation for a break-in and phone-tapping at the Democratic National Committee headquarters, in the Watergate complex. Beginning on May 18, 1973, the Watergate hearings aired live on all three major US networks. I was eleven years old and glued to the TV along with tens of millions of Americans who watched live or stayed up half the night to catch the rebroadcasts on public television.

When the Watergate hearings ended, in August, Ed had already lost or quit his job after seven years at Lincoln Hall (he never said which), and we moved to Connecticut. We bounced from one rental to another while Ed commuted back to Westchester to teach grade seven at Somers Middle School. The job came with a pay cut and a sixty-four-kilometre daily round trip in the middle of America's crushing recession and national gas shortage. In Connecticut, Pat wallpapered and sewed drapes for wealthy homeowners in Newtown, Bethel, Brookfield, and Darien.

At the end of our first year in Connecticut, Nixon resigned to avoid his inevitable impeachment. Vice-president Gerald Ford was sworn in as president, promising Americans that their "long national nightmare was over." A month later, he pardoned Nixon. President Ford's message was clear: Nixon was just a bad dream; the greatest country in the world doesn't have paranoid presidents who order criminal acts and keep enemy lists.

In 1975, I started high school. My parents bought a house on Washington Avenue in Danbury with the student loans of their older children. Danbury was a small city surrounded by prettier towns, a dreary place pocked with abandoned hat factories. If you bought a hat in the early decades of the twentieth century, it was likely made in "Hat City" by European immigrants. But the industry was already in decline: by the early 1950s, when headgear began to go out of fashion, Danbury was washed up.

After buying their new home, Ed and Pat's first act of community involvement was to sign a petition to bar a Black family from buying the house next door. Black families were largely confined to the public housing projects on Eden Drive and Laurel Gardens. Throughout the 1970s, race riots were a regular occurrence at Danbury High School, violent brawls that landed at least one student in the hospital. In 1979, fifteen years after the Civil Rights Act was passed, a member of the KKK was distributing pamphlets on the local state university campus.

I got a job as a cashier at the Danbury A&P just as Ronald Reagan resurrected the ugly myth of the welfare queen in his unsuccessful presidential run of 1976. Black families who arrived at the store with food stamps and WIC vouchers were greeted by security at the front and in the aisles. Deli cold cuts were wrapped and labelled in sets: one of three, two of three. Cashiers were told to check under Black toddlers sitting in shopping carts if three of three was missing.

By the time I hit my teens, I hadn't prayed for my parents in years. I did, however, agonize that my own moral compass was in jeopardy. Deceit—about where I was going, whom I was seeing—was required every time I wanted to leave the house. Pat insisted that my friends were laughing at me behind my back, that they were not to be trusted. Late at night, I would roll the lies I'd told over in my head like worry beads. I promised myself that there would be a day when I would tell the truth. I could be a good person.

By 1980, Reagan was elected president and the house in Danbury turned out to be a lemon. The back half was below ground level and flooded on schedule. Mushrooms sprouted in the rust-coloured shag carpet, and our family was keeping pace with the decomposition. My second and third oldest brothers were both married and divorced before they hit their late twenties. My eldest brother never returned home after attending university in Nova Scotia. My middle brother had a psychotic break and landed in the locked psych ward at Danbury Hospital. My brother's doctor recommended that Ed and Pat participate in his treatment and attend family therapy. They wouldn't risk being exposed if details about our childhoods emerged, so my brother was left on his own for three weeks at the hospital. The seven of us scrambled away from one another. In 1981, when I left to attend university in Toronto, only two of my siblings remained at home.

A few years later, it was just Pat and Ed on Washington Avenue. They opted for a second chapter. In 1984, they came to Canada and soared through the immigration process on the wings of a recently passed bill to extend funding to Catholic schools in Ontario. They rented an apartment in North York and were promptly hired by the Toronto Separate School Board (today the Toronto Catholic District School Board) as special education teachers. Pat taught the primary grades in downtown Toronto and Ed taught at a high school just around the corner from their apartment building.

Ed delighted in being the brash American with the Bronx accent and badass tattoo. His students loved him. Among the stories he liked to tell was the time he stood on his desk in a toga to teach Julius Caesar, and how he had coached the baseball team wearing the Yankees' pinstripes. Ed asked his students to help him out when school board evaluators came around during his probation period. He would ask the class a question, and every student would raise a hand. A right hand signalled that they knew the answer; a left hand would never be called on. One hundred percent participation with an astounding success rate.

Being an American in Canada was a lot easier than being one in America. I picked the best version of the American mythos and stuck with that until I couldn't. I was breezy, opinionated, and confident. In my work life and with friends, I presented my Irish American family as a sprawling, grittier version of the Kennedys playing touch football on the front lawn—only our version included parents who didn't take us to the hospital when we ended up with broken bones. The best lies are rooted in parallel truths.

I didn't stay in touch with anyone from the States outside of a few family members. And, even though they had relocated to Toronto, I didn't see much of Ed and Pat either. Instead, I settled into my Canadian life. After university, I became a landed immigrant. By the late 1980s, my work as a producer for the CBC took me to Alberta, Quebec, and Ottawa. My magazine writing took me to Saskatoon and to First Nations communities in Labrador. After my son was born, in 1991, I knew I would never live in the United States again. I couldn't imagine uprooting him—or myself, for that matter. Still, I never considered renouncing my American citizenship or formally becoming a Canadian. Occasionally, a friend would ask why, and I never had a good answer.

I didn't spend any significant time in the US again until the summer of 2001, when *Esquire* sent me to Florida to write about Nathaniel Brazill, a fourteen-year-old Black boy being tried as an adult for the fatal shooting of his white seventh-grade teacher, Barry Grunow. On the morning of May 26, 2000, Brazill had been suspended for throwing water balloons. He was sent home and returned with a handgun he had found at his grandfather's house. Brazill later told police he had just wanted to say goodbye to two girls before the school year ended. When Grunow wouldn't let him into the classroom, Brazill took the gun out to scare his teacher. As Brazill later told police, he didn't know what had happened after the gun went off. "Well, like, I couldn't see 'cause my eyes started to get real watery and stuff, so I just ran. After I seen the blood, I ran."

Brazill spent the next year awaiting trial in the Palm Beach County jail. Through the Plexiglas, I could see a whisper of hair over his top lip. He had also filled out: he was four inches taller and twenty pounds heavier. His defence attorney knew what this meant. Brazill had gone from being a boy to a "thug." His story was going to end only one way.

Brazill was convicted of second-degree murder and sentenced to twenty-eight years in prison, where he remains today. His story was in the queue for publication when the Twin Towers fell. *Esquire* held the piece. It wasn't the right time. The right time never came.

After Nathaniel Brazill and 9/11, the distance between myself and America cracked open. In the immediate aftermath of the attack, I bought an American flag and hung it on my front porch in Toronto. It was a strange impulse, a phantom-limb spasm of patriotism that I thought had been properly excised. It was also an echo of my childhood attempts at prayer, an obligation to feel what others felt.

Whatever cell memory made me hang the American flag quickly fizzled. I didn't hang the flag on the one-year anniversary of 9/11 or any year after that. What followed for America was the steady erosion of its meticulously crafted image on the world stage. A bad-faith pursuit of nonexistent weapons of mass destruction led to the disastrous foray into Iraq. At home, the Patriot Act and the Department of Homeland Security expanded the government's surveillance powers. Police departments were militarized with equipment off-loaded from the US Army—equipment used in full force today. When Americans took to their streets last spring to protest the police killing of George Floyd in Minneapolis, they were greeted by police officers straight out of *Call of Duty*: bulky monochromatic uniforms, body armour, tactical vests, flak jackets, helmets, visors, and semiautomatic assault rifles at the ready.

When I joined Facebook, in 2010, a window into the America I'd left behind opened with friend requests from my Immaculate High School class of 1979. Dozens of my Catholic schoolmates now identified as conservative evangelical Christians. I remember being unsettled by the vociferous religiosity that cluttered my Facebook feed: prayer chains, personal testimonies about God's love, and anti-abortion rhetoric. The burgeoning Canadian in me noticed that almost every American political speech ended with the command God bless America. By 2015, the conspiracy theories about Barack Obama's US citizenship had turned into misogynistic attacks on Hillary Clinton. My New Jersey cousins were vocal Trump supporters. By the summer of 2016, I'd worn out the unfriend button, and my application for Canadian citizenship was in the queue.

Trump's victory, on the evening of November 8, 2016, was a flash-bang grenade. When the country's senses came back, president-elect Donald Trump was lumbering across the stage with his family in tow. Clinton was the winner of the popular vote, with almost 66 million votes, but it didn't matter. Trump's gleefully nihilistic campaign had earned him almost 63 million votes. He'd promised a border wall, maligned Mexicans, advocated a Muslim ban, stoked violence against protestors at his rallies, threatened to jail Clinton, and bragged about sexually assaulting women. I was on the phone through much of the night and into the early morning with my middle brother in Connecticut. He'd been reassuring me for weeks that Trump didn't have a hope in hell; Clinton would mop the floor with him.

When Trump won, my brother said he'd be impeached within a year. He wasn't alone in this belief. The day after Trump's inauguration, the Women's March drew millions of protestors in cities across the country. Similar protests continued for the next two years. It seemed that many Americans could not reconcile Trump's ascendance with their ideas about America. The dissonance was profound.

On February 22, 2017, about a month after Trump's inauguration, I took my oath of Canadian citizenship along with dozens of others at Scarborough Town Centre. It was standing room only, with friends and family members of the soon-to-be new Canadians crowded together along the back and side walls, holding tiny Canadian flags. The excitement was infectious, and almost immediately, I was caught off guard by how emotional I felt. What had begun as a calculated off-ramp to unload my American citizenship had deepened into something else when I wasn't looking. The presiding judge kept things short and sweet. She congratulated us and suggested we get to know our neighbours, make new friends, and visit Canada's provincial parks.

And so it was as a Canadian that I watched the midterm elections in November 2018 and watched Trump roll back Obamacare and withdraw from the Paris Agreement. It was as a Canadian that I watched him hand out tax boons for the rich, withdraw from the Iran nuclear deal, put children in cages at the southern border, embolden violent white supremacists in Charlottesville, attack the press, shelter US enemies, and alienate allies.

While Trump napalmed the sociopolitical landscape, the mainstream media—CNN, the *New York Times*, the *Washington Post*—paddled in circles, wilfully pretending, perhaps even believing, that Trump would transform into something more presidential—that he'd stop slandering his opponents, colluding with Russians, or egging-on white supremacists. He never did. For people mortified by Trump's victory, these years were a psychic grinding of gears. Seeing but not believing. Predicting nonexistent tipping points—"This is not who we are"—and waiting for the country to be rescued by a rotating cast of heroes who never showed up: James Comey, Robert Mueller, John Kelly, James Mattis, Susan Collins, any honourable Republican.

It was a cruel political Ferberizing. But I wasn't surprised. I was watching my childhood, writ large.

With my Canadian citizenship in hand, I hired a lawyer at the end of May 2018 and slogged on with the bureaucratic waterboarding of renouncing my US citizenship. I struggled to remember exact dates and the addresses of where I had lived and worked in the United States almost four decades ago. I was unnerved by sinister warnings about the repercussions of lying or trying to evade taxes.

They demanded the highest balance in every one of my bank accounts over the past five years (Form 114a) to screen for possible money laundering. I had to provide the name and credentials of my lawyer (Form G-28). I had to fill out a Non-Resident Alien Income Tax Return for each of the past five years (Form 1040NR). With each completed form, I revealed more of myself to the American government.

To complete my formal renunciation, I was instructed to appear at the American embassy in Ottawa on October 25, 2018, at 1 pm—six months after I began the process. The embassy looks like an above-ground bunker, rising at an illusory slant and bulwarked by concrete barriers, a modern-day portcullis to prevent anybody from driving in. Cameras are mounted like turrets. The interior is muted in comparison. I was greeted outside the front door by a guard who waved a security wand over me. Inside, a second guard checked my valise and pointed me down the hall, to the cashier's wicket, to hand over my bank draft. After a short wait, Vice-counsel Angela M Mora went through my personal documents and government paperwork sheet by sheet. She then had me read and sign form DS-4081, Statement of Understanding Concerning the Consequences and Ramifications of Renunciation or Relinquishment of US Nationality. The statement reiterated warnings about tax evasion, becoming an alien, and America's power to extradite me back for a criminal offence.

Finally, the question I'd been warned about by my lawyer and by other expats who had already renounced: "Why are you choosing to renounce your citizenship today?" I had been given straightforward instructions for this exact question. I was to make it clear that I had no plans to ever work or live in the United States again and I no longer wanted to keep my citizenship. Instead, I prattled on about how I had come to love Canada. I blurted out that I didn't hate America and I might even feel sad about giving up my citizenship, but my life was in Canada now.

I was seven years old again, trying to convince myself that I loved the country I was escaping. Vice-counsel Mora looked relieved when I stopped talking. She stamped the final sheet of paper before confiscating my passport.

I renounced my American citizenship so I could stop lying, about my family and about America. The cherry-picked mythos of my American childhood that I'd imported with me to Canada didn't hold up over time. It didn't hold up with my siblings either. A brutish childhood is a burdensome thing to have in common. One of my brothers tells people his whole family died in a tragic plane crash. I appreciate the economy of his solution. Another brother simply disappeared. My family fled to three different countries and two continents.

The shortest distance between any two of us was a five-hour drive we never made.

President Joe Biden ran a successful campaign on the myth of the American character. He promised the American people that he would restore the nation's soul as well as its standing at home and abroad. He called Trump's presidency an "aberrant moment in time" and reassured exhausted voters that it wasn't too late to turn things around for the country.

More than 81 million Americans voted for Biden, the most votes a candidate has won in any American election. Trump garnered the second highest number of votes, almost 74 million—nearly 10 million more than he won four years ago. By any calculation, this election was not a repudiation of Trump or his policies. His 2016 declaration was prophetic: "I could stand in the middle of Fifth Avenue and shoot somebody, and I wouldn't lose voters." Trump is the end-stage manifestation of America's malignant self-deception. Biden's victory doesn't change this diagnosis, and his job got harder. On January 6, Trump fortified his supporters with another helping of lies about a stolen election, then watched them storm the Capitol Building, an attack that has so far claimed five lives and telegraphed America's wounds around the world.

In a nation riven by racial pain, discrimination, violence, and poverty, the biggest threat is not what divides Americans but what they have in common: the abiding lie that America is the greatest country in the world.

In 1991, my sister wrote a letter to Ed and Pat from England. In it, she catalogued the horrors of her childhood and the shadow it cast over her present. I got a copy of the letter at the same time and dreaded what might happen next. I didn't hear from either Pat or Ed, and a week later, I got a call from a police officer telling me my father was dead. I assumed Ed had killed himself. It wasn't until I got to Scarborough General Hospital, where my mother was waiting, that I learned he had died of a heart attack. He was sixty-two.

Ed had hidden the letter from Pat. My second oldest brother told me I had to find it before it killed Pat as well. After the funeral, my siblings went home to England, Vancouver, Ottawa, Chicago, California, and Connecticut. (There were fewer of us together in the same room when my mother died, in 2003.) It was just Pat and me and my six-week-old son left in Toronto. For weeks, I got regular phone calls from my brother asking if I'd located the letter. I hadn't, because I'd never looked for it.

Months after Ed's death, Pat called me, crying uncontrollably, and I knew immediately that she had found the letter. I wondered what had taken her so long. I went to see her at her apartment, in Don Mills, where we sat across from each other at the dining room table. She asked me if it was true, what my sister had written in the letter. I understood that the question was a dare; Pat didn't look away until I answered, Yes. I remember her hands resting lightly on her teacup. She looked past me, out the window, and told me she couldn't remember anything like that ever happening in our family.

THAT OTHER PLACE

Kathy Page

"Everyone who is born holds dual citizenship, in the kingdom of the well and in the kingdom of the sick," Susan Sontag wrote in *Illness as Metaphor.* "Although we prefer to use only the good passport, sooner or later each of us is obliged, at least for a spell, to identify ourselves as citizens of that other place."

The new passport has, I imagine, a charcoal grey cover. It's cheaply made and small, containing no space for visas and only a few pages of regulations written in tiny type that is illegible even when you have your glasses on. It's the opposite of the regular kind of passport in that it's entirely restrictive. It limits rather than enables travel, even the mental kind. Having such a passport compels you to devote most of your attention to observing the nature, frequency, intensity, and duration of your symptoms: *Unable to do buttons / put lid on jar / dress in leggings. Hands v. weak. Things with two hands more difficult. Tremors worse. Juddering in arms. Walk: 55 minutes . . .* I've filled several notebooks with nearly illegible, scrawled records of this kind. Such focus is necessary, yet it's also destructive in the way it monopolizes the mind: the huge, rich, complex world beyond one's body and immediate environment fades at times into a vaguely realized backdrop, a view of something now beyond reach.

First, there was an injury. In late March of 2019, running downhill on a mountain trail, I tripped on a rock. My right hand probably saved me from breaking my neck, but the impact fractured two fingers and mashed up the tissues, which understandably reacted with swelling, bruises, and pain. Experts warned the hand might take a year to *settle*. The longstanding pain in my right arm and shoulder worsened, and despite physiotherapy, computer use grew increasingly difficult. My signature and handwriting, normally fluid and large, became smaller, spikier, less controllable—*elderly*, somehow. I had a busy year touring with a new novel and noticed this especially when signing books after readings. Naturally, I blamed the injury.

Following my fall, I had to suspend yoga and swimming, and I became a left-handed gardener, but I continued to hike and still sometimes jogged the easier trails. Then, in late February 2020—just before the Covid pandemic began—I was halfway up the same mountain when I developed an odd burning sensation in my chest. After a few more such episodes I was ambulanced to the cardiac unit. The diagnosis was viral myocarditis (inflammation of the heart), *not* a heart attack, but still, the recovery period was several months. I noticed a peculiar slowness in carrying out ordinary tasks and assumed it would go away as my strength came back. My walking seemed odd, too, tight and unnatural, and I was hyper aware of changes in surface and gradient, but after all, I had been through a lot.

A tremor began in my right hand and arm.

"I think this is an *intentional* tremor," the resident standing in for my regular doctor told me at the end of a very thorough, masked appointment. Her eyes smiled as she spoke. "It's not there when your arm is relaxed. *Not* the kind that comes with Parkinson's disease." It felt like good news. My own doctor, on her return, agreed.

"Though you can have both," a poet friend told me. "That's what happened with my dad."

By the fall, I did indeed have both, and I knew that the odd slowness I was still experiencing had another name, *bradykinesia*, and was a well-known symptom of Parkinson's disease—and that small, cramped handwriting, *micrographia*, was another. Everything to do with movement and co-ordination was rapidly getting worse and I was terrified, but as my doctor stressed, other explanations were still possible. It could be viral. It could be some kind of nerve damage from the fall. It could be medication-related. It could be MS, and that might show up on an MRI ... I had definitely crossed into the kingdom of the sick, but despite my doctor's efforts, I was still waiting for both the MRI and for an appointment with the neurologist, and so no one was willing to actually diagnose me. I started on anti-depressants and squared up to the wait.

A new grey passport brings new responsibilities. When you inhabit the kingdom of the sick, it is your job to understand then explain your disease, and the medical and bureaucratic systems it has forced you to be part of. You must learn a new vocabulary and teach it to those you love and those you are obliged to inform. Relaying to family, friends, and doctors the details and sensations of one's condition, along with various medical opinions, opaque test results, etc., not to speak of the emotional consequences of all of it, is at times a huge relief—yet it can soon become time-consuming and repetitive—doubtless for listeners too, though of course, there are those who care deeply, and others who have a curiosity about such things, as well as quite a few who enjoy the feeling of *schadenfreude*. (This last is merely an observation: I don't begrudge it them.)

Virginia Woolf, describing in her 1930 essay *On Being Ill*, "the undiscovered countries" of sickness, was frank about the impossibility of understanding another's suffering. She noted that "Human beings do not go hand in hand the whole stretch of the way. There is a virgin forest in each; a snowfield where even the print of birds' feet is unknown. Here we go alone and like it better so." I love the prose but resist the final clause. Communication may be difficult and imperfect, yet I yearn for it.

Even pre-Covid, when you could actually *be* with someone instead of seeing them on a blurry, freezing screen or just hearing their telephone voice, it was a challenge to fully enter into another person's lived physical reality. Now, separated from each other, it is much harder. Add to that a long period of not having a clear diagnosis, seeming fairly coherent while actually falling apart, and a reputation for health and vigor—misunderstanding is almost guaranteed. And of course, it is only natural that most listeners reach desperately for an experience of their own as comparison, though it may bear very little likeness other than that it concerns a physical dysfunction of some kind.

Still, it can feel wearing—even upsetting—to listen for forty-five minutes to a friend telling you of a miracle cure experienced for an entirely different ailment, or else relaying the details of a highly speculative, possibly-one-day-to-be-cutting-edge treatment for what you are experiencing, one that is however unproven and not available to you for at least ten years and then only at enormous cost in another country. But remember: A citizen of the kingdom of the sick needs to develop patience and good manners.

The speaker means well. They too are in shock. Your news is unpleasant, and they want to offer something, to kindle hope, to help in some way. What they are telling you is the best or first thing that came to mind. And somewhere, buried in it, may lie a nugget of useful information (or not). Remind yourself of this as your arm begins to shake from holding the phone. You will need your friends. Later, perhaps, you will learn how to take gentle control of such conversations.

Actually no, I have said many times, striving for a warm but authoritative tone, it's *not* my heart. That problem back in March was viral myocarditis and it's all better. This is new. It's neurological. It's an as yet undiagnosed "movement disorder," so hands, arms, legs, muscles in general, and of course the brain—I feel as if I am moving though water. Or as if I'm trying to drive a faulty machine. Or as if a spell has been cast over me. Nothing is ordinary or works as it should and there is no ease or relief, except in sleep. I can't work; I'm on sick leave from the university ... *No,* I'm not writing, and *yes,* I do know I must self-advocate. I have really tried. I update the doctor every week. I have spoken at length with several very pleasant and ultimately unyielding medical receptionists. The system, underfunded, always slow, is now backed up due to the Covid-19 shut-down in the spring. Neurologists are scarce as snakes' hair. Sick people are everywhere, begging for attention; I have no idea when I will see a specialist or have a diagnosis but am told it will be months rather than weeks, and in any case, not until next year.

Meanwhile, I take five minutes to tie my shoelaces, then walk slower than I'd like to for an hour. Judder my way through some recommended exercises every morning (effortful, slow). Try not to be utterly useless in the house. Eat—often with a spoon as it is easier. Answer email using occasionally hilarious error-prone dictation software. Talk to doctors and friends. Read. Time both creeps and rushes by.

The summer has been cooler than usual but towards the end of August the air thickens with the stench of forest fires in Washington and Oregon to the south of us. Thousands flee their homes. The Arctic melts. Covid numbers surge. It's impossible to ignore the rabid roar of right-wing mobs. RBG dies. Then there's the long, horrifying run-up to the US election. Conditions in my body and out there in the world both seem pretty bad. But some things help. It helps that at night I lie warm and dry in bed next to the one I love, and that by day we eat the garden's greens, beans, beets, squash, carrots; we listen to its noisy birds, savour the sun and gaze at yearning blue skies ... It helps to notice the many kinds of clouds. Mist. Rain. White rock and viridian conifer. The shimmering of rippled ocean, absolutely clear, pulled up tight over a pebble beach. Ravens calling to each other in flight. The mother deer and two speckled fawns. The moon. The way shooting stars zip up the inky sky.

My husband writes me a song. He and my son help with newly difficult simple things. My sister, my best writer friend, and my editor phone regularly to check in and cheer me up—others call, or pick up, just at the right moment and don't mind settling in for the hour. I have long talks with kind strangers, the friends or acquaintances of friends, ready to offer information, contacts, ideas. Local friends seem happy to accommodate my new awkwardness and walk with me on the mountains, in the park, by the sea—always with trees nearby. Neighbours share a jellied treat, *Birsalma sajt* (Hungarian) aka *Membrillo* (Spanish), made from yellow quince; they bring jam, relish, brown bags of garden apples and perfect pears.

I'm given fitness programs, computer advice, osteopathic treatments. Bags of books and lists of titles to hunt down. A cashmere scarf in blues, greens and pink, another purple and gold, another light as air in dark subtle shades. Thoughtful emails, (terrible) jokes, and sudden tears. Paper letters folded inside hand-made cards. A thick woollen cardigan, a workbook on constructive thinking. I'm offered recommendations, advice, acknowledgement, encouragement, patience, and, where possible during a pandemic, real as well as virtual kisses.

Knowing that I am in others' thoughts—that I even appear in their dreams—warms and sustains me. And there's more:

schadenfreude's sweet, lesser-known opposite, for which there is no German word. Fortunately, Sanskrit offers *Mudita*: sympathetic joy, the pleasure that comes from delighting in other people's well-being.

And so, while symptoms do persist and worsen—and a tiny orange blob smoulders in what used to September's sky—I enjoy our son's happiness with his first ever vehicle, an elderly orange truck. I'm happy because a formerly sad teacher-friend of mine retired, took up wild swimming and seems reborn. I think of a frustrated artist now building a studio in her garden, and of my widowed journalist neighbour, giddily in love. Two other friends, a couple almost-divorced, back together. One writer's risky eye surgery is safely completed; another's novel, eight years in the making, is finally being read and loved. Yet another has a story shortlisted for a prize. Then there's my sister! Thriving and happy in New Zealand. My nephew did not die in the accident. His leg will heal.

Mudita, mudita! Tell me your good news, I say, when people call. Bring it on. I'm not jealous. Don't be shy! I hoard such joys as if they were a bowl of the mottled pink and purple bean seeds from overgrown scarlet runners, the beans my daughter as a child used to call magic beans. I touch each in turn, feel the warmth of the sun that made them and find solace in that same daughter, now twenty-four, how she loves her new job.

In the buttery autumn light, the last of it perhaps, a bookseller friend and I sit in person (distanced) outside. I have given her the full narrative of my fall and cascading symptoms; she now tells me the history of her hip, which, we note, also begins with a fall: leaving the organic food store next door to her own premises, she trod on an acorn which rolled beneath her foot. Initially this tipped her backwards. Instinct told her not to go that way and dash the back of her head on the pavement. She swung her arms forwards—each was laden with a heavy cloth bag—briefly righted herself, but then crashed forwards onto her hands and knees. Apples, carrots, and potatoes spilled from her bags. The fall grazed one set of knuckles and one palm, but her right knee and hip absorbed most of the impact. Both grew more painful in the ensuing weeks, making walking, sitting, standing, and turning into a set of inescapable agonies. A year of physiotherapy followed; it was early on in that time that her husband decided to leave her, though later, he changed his mind.

Recovery would be a slow process, she was warned, and thirteen months on, she still has difficulty walking, sitting, and standing. The lining of the hip joint is suspect, as are all the tendons and muscles surrounding it. The physiotherapist recently raised the spectre of something called *internal derangement*: a muscle may have lost its proper place and if so, can only be fixed, and only possibly, by a very risky surgery.

We two fallen women eat a bowl of just-picked plums and laugh about *internal derangement*. Deranged is something we both feel right now. We compare it to my *intentional tremor*, which sounds to the uninitiated as if I'm shaking on purpose, a thing that could not be further from the truth. We agree that the *tremor at rest* I also have seems like a contradiction in terms. We speculate as to the possibility of *intentional derangement*.

It's extraordinarily good to be able to laugh about being sick.

And so long as you can do so, and can bear to take fair turns, the company of other sick people is very comforting, though it can be overwhelming and exhausting too. Making comparisons is potentially dangerous—but we two are old friends and agree, after some debate, that my condition is likely worse than hers, nasty as that is. Both are disabling, but mine seems likely to be *progressive* (another strange word, given the meaning is that it inexorably gets worse), incurable and life-abbreviating. This may make her feel relatively fortunate, but I don't ask.

After my friend's visit, I remember something that predates my own fall by several years and may be the real beginning of what is happening to me.

I'd set a pan of rice to cook. Sitting not far away, I was soon absorbed in editing some short stories, and only eventually looked up and *saw* smoke; I smelled nothing, even though the pan had burnt to black at the bottom. Extensive tests ruled out a brain tumour and various other possibilities; a specialist diagnosed rhinitis.

She did not mention, though, that loss of the sense of smell, *anosmia,* can be an early sign of Parkinson's disease. The information came up online, but I had no other symptoms, so put the knowledge aside and then forgot it. Life was busy on all fronts: teaching, writing, family, garden. I biked, hiked, and swam. Just six months before my fall, I completed a mountainous hiking tour at altitude in Peru. I chaired the Creative Writing department, published a new book of stories, a novel ...

"Do you think my loss of smell could be significant?" I ask my doctor during the next phone appointment.

"It could be," she says, "but the neurologist will be the best person to ask."

"The unattainable neurologist."

She joins me in a brittle little laugh.

There is paperwork, and another special dialect to learn:

> In some cases, where appropriate, services of our rehabilitation specialist are requested to work with the employee and their employer to assist in a return to meaningful employment; we will advise you should such services be appropriate. We will continue to request regular updates

from you. We will contact you to obtain an update on your progress and treatment plans.

You have responsibilities that are key to the management of your claim. It is expected that you will make reasonable efforts to participate in reasonable treatment and rehabilitation, advise us of any changes in your condition, work towards returning to your own occupation, or assist in identifying other suitable employment, and/ or accept reasonable offers of alternate or modified work from your employer.

I note three *reasonables* in one sentence, along with a *suitable*, but this is not for me to point out. I do know how fortunate I am to have even such grudging support, but yes, I miss producing and playing with words.

Anxious, unable to sleep, I lie on my back in the inky dark and think of my family and friends. What can I do for them? Often the answer is not very much at all—but even the smallest thing feels good. One writer friend recommends a book called *How to Do Nothing*. I joke that I am doing it rather well. You sound too stoical, she says.

Stoical? If so it's a public face. On my own, at home, it's different. Tears streamed down my face when my doctor suggested on the phone that my symptoms might be virally induced and so there was at least a chance that they might therefore resolve, given time.

These were tears of sheer gratitude at the possibility of getting better, of release from one story into another somewhat-possibly better one. Later, my husband and I cried together when we admitted to ourselves that "the golden virus" idea was a mirage . . . And then I cried alone in the woods, thinking how much my relationship with my husband has changed and will change, how it is becoming one where he helps and looks after me more than formerly and I am no longer a powerful equal in our life together, but a dependent. I cried for both of us. I asked him would he need someone else more functional to keep him sane? No, he said, of course not; more tears ensued.

I sobbed when I felt alone with all the unpleasant information I was acquiring and hoarding so as to avoid overwhelming those close to me. Most recently, I howled when I could not do a simple piece of foot-and-arm co-ordination in an online exercise class—it was a small pain that stood in for everything—I gushed, wailed, doubled over in the face of this momentary humiliation, of my new powerlessness, of the many losses. There was rage, fear, and desperation. My husband came to comfort me; my son, three rooms away and wearing headphones to participate in an online seminar, did not hear a thing. It felt good to cry without restraint.

I'm no stoic, but you can't be howling all the time.

It's important to remember that people who ask, "But are you doing *your own work?*" are just trying to understand. But the question does seem preposterous. They are asking whether, despite being mysteriously dysfunctional in many different, aforementioned ways, and so unable to teach, whether I am somehow capable of functioning as a novelist, i.e., doing one of the most exciting but also most demanding things there is, along with associated administrative and publicising tasks. As Haruki Murakami puts it in *What I Talk About When I Talk About Running*:

> Writing novels, to me, is basically a kind of manual labor. Writing itself is mental labor, but finishing an entire book is closer to manual labor ... Most people, though, only see the surface reality of writing and think of writers as involved in quiet, intellectual work done in their study. If you have the strength to lift a coffee cup, they figure, you can write a novel. But once you try your hand at it,

you soon find that it isn't as peaceful a job as it seems. The whole process—sitting at your desk, focusing your mind like a laser beam, imagining something out of a blank horizon, creating a story, selecting the right words, one by one, keeping the whole flow of the story on track—requires far more energy, over a long period, than most people ever imagine ... there's grueling, dynamic labor going on inside you. Everybody uses their mind when they think. But a writer puts on an outfit called narrative and thinks with his entire being; and for the novelist that process requires putting into play all your physical reserve, often to the point of overexertion ...

It's painful to explain over and over that it takes me at least four times as long as normal to clean my teeth or get my pants on. That I need to *think through* how to turn a tee shirt the right way out and put the correct but mysteriously juddering and trembling arm through the appropriate sleeve, and so perhaps it is not surprising that, leaving aside my current lack of energy and ideas, I'm unable to write normally even in the purely mechanical sense. Better dictation software *might* help somewhat with some of what I need to do but is not a panacea.

I think there's some residual romanticism behind the notion that "own work" might be possible when one is falling apart—a belief that a real writer will and should be driven, no matter what the obstacles, to use their last ounce of energy to write. Some might, of course. And it's completely understandable that my friends to see writing novels as a fundamental to my identity. Until recently I felt that way too, but very quickly, like any new citizen here in the other place, I have been forced to imagine otherwise, and to renegotiate the possible.

If I had an idea in my head, maybe I could write a haiku now and then. A page long moment-story in a month or two. I'd be happy to manage either of these. I'm writing this, of course, at a rate of about three lines a day.

Living here, one must learn how to be far less productive. It's very hard to do, but also interesting: Who am I really? What's essential? How much can be subtracted from what I am used to being and doing without the obliteration of what I think of as "me"? Will I notice or care if "I" do vanish? Without writing, can I sustain a sense of value and purpose, or must I learn to live without that? I have no answers yet.

Eventually there is a cold ferry ride and then a long drive, through rain and mist. The clinic this doctor works from is by far the busiest place in a down-at-heel, half-deserted mall. The receptionist warns that the doctor always runs late, and he does, almost an hour. But I don't care. It's a real, face-to-face appointment.

He's a short man, middle aged. We're both medically masked, of course, he at his desk in a corner facing the wall and I seated so that I see him from the side. Exhibiting several of them as I do so, I catalogue my symptoms as calmly and economically as possible. He studies the referral letter intently as I speak. Yet he somehow listens and eventually he looks, examines, puts me through some tests, and then, to my surprise, helps me get my shoes back on for a walk down the corridor and back.

"You do have several symptoms of Parkinson's disease," he confirms as he settles back into his chair. "Your walking, tremors and slowness are the most noticeable."

He advises that the best next step is to take a medication called carbidopa levodopa. If it works, and he thinks it will, the diagnosis is confirmed. He writes a bloodwork requisition and a prescription: I should take a slowly increasing dose over a month or so to determine the appropriate amount and then continue for another two months to see how stable my response is, and whether any side effects are tolerable.

It's a smallish pill, oval, yellow. I already know a bit about it. Levodopa or L-dopa, the main ingredient, has been around since the late 1960s. It's a synthetic precursor to the neuro-transmitter dopamine. The brain can use it to make the dopamine that dying or degenerating neurons in areas called the *basal ganglia* and the *substantia nigra* no longer produce. Dopamine makes you feel good; more importantly it enables and regulates movement; the lack of it causes all sorts of problems.

I notice I write here almost casually of "the brain," but of course, I think not "the," but "my." Parts of *my* brain are degenerating in a process that is mysterious, terrifying, irreversible, and unstoppable. The news, even if expected, is hard to absorb and I am, to begin with, oddly calm.

Like many people, I have heard about Levodopa because Oliver Sacks wrote about it in his extraordinary book, part memoir, part study, *Awakenings*. There, he explains how an epidemic of *encephalitis lethargica*, or "sleepy sickness," infected thousands of people worldwide in the 1920s, leaving many with permanent, very severe Parkinson's-like symptoms. Largely immobile, dazed and seemingly apathetic, these survivors were cared for over decades in dedicated wards and institutions, several of which Sacks visited in the 1960s.

In 1969, when the price of the new dopamine-supplementing drug called L-Dopa became affordable, Sacks prescribed it to a group of eighty *encephalitis lethargica* patients who had existed in a kind of spellbound condition for four decades inside a New York hospital. The effect varied from patient to patient, but often was swift and quasi miraculous, with patients quickly waking from their long somnolence to experience the joys of movement and communication. During the past decades they had apparently been aware of their environment and situation, yet unable or not motivated to respond; now life could begin again. In a 1985 interview on NPR, Sacks later described witnessing this transformation as "like seeing frozen figures thawing and with this a great delight as an awakening or sort of resurrection might be expected to have."

But amazing as the results were, problems soon developed. Awake, and sometimes even hyperalert, the patients were in many ways still the young people they had been when they became lethargic; since that point they'd had no new experiences, missed out on normal life and formed very few new memories. They had not really grown, changed or aged. Many were without family or friends. As well as that, the drug had inconsistencies and unwanted effects which many found intolerable.

In the end, very few of the patients' stories shared by Sacks have happy endings, though some do.

The use of Levodopa has been somewhat refined since *Awakenings* was written, but the treatment for Parkinson's has, like Sacks' lethargic patients, been in a fairly static state for many years. The same synthetic dopamine precursor is still the main drug prescribed, though it is now often combined with carbidopa, an enhancement that prevents the Levodopa being broken down before it crosses the blood-brain barrier and is made into useable dopamine; the benefit of this is that some unwanted effects may be slower to appear and the dose of Levodopa can be smaller, which is important, since—as with the original—the effect of dopamine replacement on a Parkinson's patient can be miraculous in its initial transformative and liberating effects, and yet, as the disease progresses and as higher and more frequent doses are required, for most people it becomes over time increasingly problematic and decreasingly effective.

Towards the end of the consultation, I call my husband into the consulting room and provide a precis.

"I won't hold you to it, but how long do you think it will work for me?" I ask the oddly unexpressive and yet, I sense, fundamentally compassionate doctor.

"Everyone is different—" He meets my gaze for what seems like the first time. "It's useful for . . . a number of years. Typically, between six and fifteen . . . I will say though that your symptoms seem to have been developing quickly rather than slowly."

He closes the cardboard file on his desk and hands me the prescription and a requisition for blood work.

"It's very hard to know what to do," my husband says. "We need to downsize. I'd like to get our ducks in a row, but—"

"I wouldn't advise you to make any big decisions until we've done this trial. I'll see you again in April," he adds. Another appointment already. I won't forget that he fitted me in to an already bursting schedule.

"If I need to, may I ask questions on the phone?" I ask.

"I'll try to respond," he says. "But I'm busy. I always run late."

In the seating area beyond the consulting room, other patients sit spaced, masked, eyes glazed. Outside, the mist has turned to rain; concrete, asphalt and sky are darkening their greys.

"How do you feel?" my husband asks once we are in the car.

"Hungry," I tell him struggling to remove the lid from the jar of nuts we brought with us. "Well, I'm not delighted," I tell him. And certainly, I could be feeling better (Doc said he's seen this before, and it passes), or I could be feeling worse (if, say, he'd thought that I have Multiple System Atrophy, or Supra Nuclear Palsy). "He gave the impression he's pretty sure I have Parkinson's, and I don't want to have it. But since I suspected it anyway, being seen, spoken to honestly, and given some kind of potential treatment is a step forward ..." The almost-knowledge we now have is not welcome, but it is better than being in anxious limbo, shaking and juddering, untreated, and suspecting the very same thing.

"Yes," my husband says, and he starts the car, turns up the fan. The windscreen is fogged up and the rain—noisy now—falls thick and fast. "That's pretty much it."

Half a yellow pill three times a day is just to connect body and drug, and expose any unwelcome effects. It's not expected to be enough. Even so, something happens. The effects are subtle, yet definitely present: tremor is subdued, if still lurking. Steadier hands, a greater feeling of physical calmness. Perhaps my walking is a little better? Some things seem somewhat easier to do, others not—there's a taste of honey, at least. At the end of the ten days, I double the dose and within the day comes real sweetness. To begin with, I hardly dare to speak of it, and in any case, how can I describe this loosening of my bonds to someone who has not suffered months of restriction and feeling bewitched?

I'm moving more freely, walking almost normally. Everything's easier—but far more than that—everything is a pleasure. Imagine: taking the stairs two at a time. Reaching to the high shelf. Opening a door. Almost slamming it. Pouring water from a jug. Holding a full cup in one hand. Emptying the dishwasher: swoop down—up—reach—twist—slot plates in the rack, and all without being continuously aware that I used to do this better and something terrible is wrong with me. Ordinary movements are a kind of dance—and who cares that dancing is something I've never been good at? This is it, here I am!

I feel as if I have sneaked back across the border into the kingdom of the well. I slip my arms at almost normal pace into my jacket, zip it up at only the second attempt, competently tie my shoelaces, then stride out into the world. Yes, I do still have to remind myself to swing my arms, but less often than before; they swing higher and faster, and my left hand is not twitching, not at all. I walk downhill, uphill, on the flat; I walk fast and hard and savour every step, sometimes break into a skip or a jog . . . When my artist friend and I reach the viewpoint just before the summit of the mountain, it is ice and snow on the trail, not fatigue, that prevent us from continuing to the top. I'm certain we'll get there next week. Meanwhile, wind combs our hair as we absorb the silvery sea, the profusion of islands, the infinite hues of a blue-grey sky.

Because my body is more freely moving and does not claim my attention, my mind is liberated, too. I notice and think about things other than my own sensations and situation. Anything. Everything. It's all there. As Sacks puts it in *Awakenings*, albeit writing about patients far deeper into their disease than I have yet travelled in mine:

"The awakened patient . . . falls in love with reality itself . . . Where, previously, she felt ill at ease, uncomfortable, unnatural, and strained, she now feels at ease and at one with the world. All aspects of her being—her movements, her perceptions, her thoughts, and her feelings—testify simultaneously to the fact of awakening. The stream of being, no longer clogged or congealed, flows with an effortless unforced ease . . . There is a great sense of spaciousness or freedom of being. The instabilities and knife edges of disease disappear, and are replaced by poise, resilience, and ease." (I'm aware that *ease* is used four times, but it is a lovely word.)

These feelings, Sacks writes, "show us the full quality—the zenith of real being (so rarely experienced by most healthy people); they show us what we have known—and almost forgotten; what all of us once had—and have subsequently lost."

I have re-read his book; I've studied the ongoing research online. I know that my visa is a temporary one, that this current bliss won't last for ever, but I refuse to dwell on that, except to note that right now impermanence makes its flavour yet more complex and intense.

"If only we could have a party!" I tell my husband, and kiss him on the neck as he—not knowing, as I now do, that to do so is a miracle—touches fingers to keys and makes words appear on a screen.

A MAN, WITHOUT

Chafic LaRochelle

> But that's the way of the world.
>
> — Homer's *Odyssey* (Book XIX, line 190)

When I was ten, my father sat me down for a talk.

We were in the kitchen. A bright room, sparsely furnished, with a naked fluorescent bulb humming overhead. The sink dripped in rhythmic *plops* and, once in a while, the pipes gurgled irritably, as though roused from some groggy slumber. Upstairs, the neighbours raced thoroughbreds—or so it seemed; their *thumps* and *thuds* sent tremors down our walls and through the crusty dishes that littered the countertop. But despite the *hums*, *plops*, *gurgles*, *thumps*, *thuds*, and *clinks*, silence enveloped us.

We sat facing each other on a pair of aluminium chairs. The seat's lipstick-red upholstery was torn and uncomfortable, the plastic sticky with dried sweat and dust. I could feel his eyes on me, but my own eyes were fixed on a hole in my sweatpants. He cleared his throat. I didn't look up.

Why had he called me into the kitchen—a place for morning papers, long-distance phone calls, and unrequited scratch tickets? Something in his voice had spooked me. Maybe it was the foreign note of uncertainty it carried like a faceless vagrant, unwelcome and impenetrable. I stayed very still, waiting for him to speak, as though my stillness could alter the unfurling present. All at once his voice castrated the lofty silence.

"You're almost a man now," he said, "and being a man means doing the right thing—even when you don't want to ..." He lit a filterless cigarette and took a long drag, the tobacco hissing in weak protest as it caught ablaze. He held it in his lungs awhile before exhaling a long plume of smoke that dissipated into the hungry, yellow walls. "Especially when you don't want to," he added. "Go crack the window."

Eyes still lowered, I got up and went to the small window above the sink. The frost had made it difficult to open, so I climbed onto the counter and pulled hard on the tabs. It gave way with a weary groan that nearly toppled me into the sink; a leaning tower of plates wavered uncertainly before settling back into inertia, back into placid chaos.

"*Kess ikhtak*," he said, stroking the embers of his cigarette along the sooty lip of the ashtray. "You know I love you, *habibi*, don't you? I love you very much. That's something I've never been ashamed to say."

I could hear rogue snowflakes grazing the concrete sill. It was just outside but it sounded far away. He took one last, long draw from his cigarette and pressed it into the cinder. "Hardest thing I've ever had to do," he said quietly, nodding to himself. "Hardest thing, hardest thing ..."

This—coming from a man who'd witnessed his country fractured by civil war. A man who'd outlived his entire family. Who'd lost his fortune, then his marriage, to bad choices and worse luck. Some primitive instinct made my hairs stand on edge, as if alerting me to an imminent, though inevitable, danger. He placed a hand on my shoulder. With the other, he reached into his shirt pocket and removed a folded slip.

"This," he said, holding my gaze now, "is an eviction notice."

Occam had taken a razor to my father's life and still found the result unsatisfactory. He was a proud man, descended from bearded sailors in purple garb who navigated uncharted waters, devising numerals in the cradle of civilization . . . but that was a long time ago now, ground into fine powder by the cogs of time and scattered by a passing breeze.

After their divorce—and in spite of her own feelings—my mother had tried to explain it to me. She said it wasn't my fault. That my father suffered from "having a partial soul." A dismembered, ethereal body came to mind.

I squinted at the eviction notice.

"What does it mean?"

"It means I can't live here anymore."

My ears rang before I could untangle the meaning of his words.

"It means," he said, his voice unsteady, "that I have to go." Through clenched teeth, he asked, "Do you understand?"

I shook my head.

"Please, son," he said, "I need you to understand—tell me you do."

I tried to speak but choked, shaking my head as tears clouded my vision. All I could see was his silhouette, slouching pathetically against the harsh white light. His dark figure grew larger and larger until all was dark and I felt his arms around me, my face buried in the musky folds of his polyester button-down.

"Come, come, it's gonna be alright," he said, forcing a laugh, "of course it'll be alright." Through a wad of syrupy spit, I suggested the obvious, "Come back and live with me and mom!" But he just went on holding me, saying, "It'll be alright," his body trembling against mine.

Later, suspended in that hollow state between being broken and built anew, my father made breakfast. Eggs, scrambled, doused in salt and pepper, served with sides of sliced tomato and burnt pita bread.

He wasn't strictly making breakfast; this was just about all he knew how to cook, served at roughly the right time to be called breakfast. We ate little and spoke less. With a deep sense of Mediterranean duty, he'd encourage me to take another bite (and another, and another). But his attempts were lacklustre and wanting. From the portable stereo in the other room, John Lennon sang indistinctly about peace and unity and Christmas. My father had put it on to drown the silence, but it was too late. It had already spoken and it said, *things will never be the same.* All I managed to get down were a few runny tomato wedges.

I stared at the eviction notice. It was folded carelessly just a few inches from my plate. I picked it up, examined it, turned it over in my hands, felt its weight. When I closed my eyes I could hardly imagine that I was holding anything at all—yet these few carefully selected words, on this featherlight slip, printed and punctuated and arranged just so, had changed everything.

Stuck to the fridge beneath a *Casino de Montréal* magnet was a schedule my father had written in his steady hand. It listed the times and channels of all the sports, cartoons, and old movies we wanted to watch that week. Tonight was basketball; our job was to make sure the TV was ready.

As it happened, the building's cable box was at the end of the hall. My father would jimmy the lock with a flathead and plug us back into the grid while I stood guard by the stairs for witnesses. It always felt like it was us against the world. At the very least, it felt like it was us against the Videotron Telecommunications Company. "It's not stealing," he'd remind me. "It's too easy to be called stealing. People work a hundred times harder for a bucket of water. That's just the way of the world."

But tonight, after a dinner of canned chilli and more burnt pita, he simply handed me the flathead and went to wash the dishes. It was an unexpected gesture, an act of defeat. I think he was trying to prepare me for his absence. Teach me about responsibility, about growing up, and about stealing cable from the Videotron Telecommunications Company.

I plugged us into the grid then sat down on the derelict marble stairs and wept. When I returned, he was packing his few possessions into heavy-duty garbage bags: dishes, CDs, VHS cassettes, some clothing, some bed linen. The only real furnishings he owned were the TV set and its melamine stand. Everything else was either already in the apartment or acquired in some vague, moneyless way.

He found the couch on our street one afternoon during garbage collection. Since he couldn't carry it alone he spent the day roosting on the building stoop, chainsmoking and reading through every section of *The Gazette*, from breaking news to obituaries. When at last the garbage truck arrived, he convinced the men to walk it up the five flights to his apartment. It's a testament to his persuasiveness, because they didn't even ask for compensation.

I remember the way they looked at me as they left. One of them was a skinny French-Canadian, with facial piercings and faded green-black tattoos crawling up the sides of his neck. The other was a sturdy Haitian man, older, with a weathered face and russet eyes; he leaned in and offered me a strawberry candy with an uncertain smile. The Quebecois, waiting for my father to be out of earshot, whispered, "Just keep an eye out for those bedbugs, *tabarnak*."

That couch had been a good friend to my father, a trusted companion. He'd often fall asleep on it just before dawn while the TV played white noise on loop. I mostly avoided it, however, because merely being in its presence aroused a particle cloud so inconceivable that it demanded ten sneezes. Besides, the material had the consistency of an oily cat in its final, cancerous days.

But my father didn't mind the dust. He didn't even mind the look of it: swaths of alloy green and metallic purple on an olive and black background. The colours would change as you moved across the room from one vantage point to another, giving it an unattractive holographic quality—and further enhancing the oily-cat effect.

I spent the night at his place. He let me have the queen-size mattress we used to wrestle on and claimed the oily couch for himself. For all that had happened, I had no trouble sleeping.

When I woke up, my mother was waiting for me in the kitchen, on the same lipstick-red chair where I'd sat the day before. She was across from my father but they faced away from one another in a silence that was both comfortable and contemptuous, using their lips only to smoke. My father with his natives and my mother her filtered menthols.

"Gather your belongings," she said dryly, tapping her nails against the laminate tabletop.

At the door my father hugged me for a long time, planting kisses on my hair, my forehead. "I'm sorry," he kept saying, "for all of it. It'll make sense when you're older. I pray that it will. Just be patient and I'll come for you, *habibi*. Soon as everything's sorted."

He peered down his aquiline nose, as if weighing my understanding. His eyes had that lazy, calculating look of a desert merchant appraising a rare jewel in the quiet of a still noon. They were deep brown, like coffee with a splash of milk—the pitiful remains of a nearly expired carton. Now those keen Phoenician eyes appeared to say, *I live my life by the whims of the sea; my home is nowhere.*

That was the last time I stepped foot into a place my father called home.

Years passed before the dust settled. When it did, the mirage of a life restored was gone for good. In its place was a single thread, thin and fragile, dangling between an awkward teenage boy and a weary old man. We'd meet every so often at a downtown café for a game of chess. We never spoke of the lost years.

The café was a haven for old, nostalgic men who'd all fled the Fertile Crescent for one reason or another. Now in their life's twilight, the men collected their pensions and met daily to bicker over world affairs, religious doctrine, and the young girls from the fashion college across the street. They pumped their veins with caffeine and nicotine and passed the hours cheating each other out of small bets over rowdy backgammon games.

My father, middle-aged and greying but still young for the crowd, would make an appearance whenever he needed money. He was unbeatable. In his late-twenties, he had prospered as a Vegas backgammon champ—one of the many ways he had managed to become rich, if only briefly. Such was his knack for making money, however bad he was at keeping it.

Even though he routinely took them for all they had, they adored him. They saw him not only as the Lebanese Bobby Fischer, but as a valuable interpreter between Middle Eastern and North American culture. Unlike them, talk of his homeland never elicited a glassy-eyed, thousand-mile stare followed by a flood of positive adjectives.

Talk of his homeland was not something he did at all. He never volunteered anything about those days and answered evasively whenever asked. "Beirut was once considered the Switzerland of the Middle East," was the most I ever heard him say on it before quickly changing the subject. The Old Arabs teased him, calling him a man without a country.

What they didn't know was that he was also a man without a god.

He grew up in a big family in Beirut. It was a loving home, where Nat King Cole and Ray Charles were frequent guests

and the stovetop was always warm. My father was the young-
est of five brothers. They'd spend their weekends loitering in
the park, shooting hoops with whoever was around. In the
evenings, they'd say grace and share stories about their day
over a hot communal meal.

During the week, my father attended a Jesuit school. He
was a gifted student, fluent in three languages, able to solve
complex arithmetic problems in his head, and sometimes
even on time for class. He played point guard on the high
school basketball team and had a sock drawer full of medals
to prove it.

On weekends, his eldest brother would take him downtown
to see the latest spaghetti western or Burt Lancaster picture. My
father would run out of the theatre, pointing finger pistols at
passersby, taking cover behind parked cars, pretending to be
Hollywood's latest and greatest cowboy stud. His brother would
play along, chasing him down the main drag. When he'd finally
catch him, he would spank his ass and holler about how cute
it was, sending my mortified father running all the way home.

I imagine that's when life was best. I see him as an outgoing
young man, in skin-tight acid-wash bell-bottoms, buying up
the newest Bee Gees vinyl from the local record shop, barhop-
ping in search of dimpled, olive-skinned girls flashing shy
grins … It's a vivid portrait but if I ever met that man I wouldn't
recognize him. Sometimes I wonder if he felt the same.

I don't know much about the days after life stopped
being like that. But once, shortly before they divorced, I over-
heard him talking to my mom about it. He'd been drinking
and came home very late and very broke from a foray at the
casino. After a small argument followed by a meek apology,
he started to ramble about losing money and why you can't
ever trust people. Then he said to her, "One day you're playing basketball at the park with the whole neighbourhood, the
next you're playing tag with live rounds of gunfire, wondering
who's friend and who's foe. And for what?

"For red team or blue team—team Mohammed or team Jesus. You know something? Every religion's a cult of human sacrifice. You learn that when you see your best friend's brains blown out, lying in the arms of his shrieking, blood-soaked mother, wondering why—why and where did she go wrong? Didn't she pray hard enough? Didn't she carry her sins with enough shame? It's fucking madness, *kess ikhtak*, when man confuses his ego for his spirit." Though muffled and quiet, I could hear them both crying through the thin wall. "And yet," said my mother finally, "life continues."

Time passed and the war dragged on interminably. What had initially caught everyone off-guard was now ubiquitous; bombs fell, bullets flew, and life did continue. Women still went to the market to buy produce and exchange gossip, men still cursed the rush-hour traffic, and children played hide-and-seek in the skeletons of exploded buildings.

But my father had had enough. He packed a bag and said a long goodbye to his family. Though he didn't know it then, that was the last time he would see them. And the last time he'd ever set foot in a place he called home.

He took his sock drawer full of medals and left god behind in the ashes of his burning country.

Between games of chess he'd step outside for a cigarette. I'd reset the board then usually read until he came back. Other times, I'd just watch him through the window as he stood there smoking, lost in thought. His face would change when he was alone; the lines around his mouth would deepen and his eyes cast a faraway look. Was he dissecting the past? Trying to pinpoint the precise moment when he had become a stranger to himself?

At some point in his reverie, he'd reach into his shirt pocket and remove a folded slip of paper, much like the one from all those years ago. He would stare at it quizzically then pull a pen from his pocket and hastily scribble something down. Every time it happened, my curiosity grew—I had to know what great epiphany had compelled him to commit words to paper.

One day I arrived early to the cafe. The Old Arabs welcomed me emphatically as I walked past them to our usual table at the back by the window. The chess board was already set up, but my father's chair was empty.

"In the bathroom," said the owner, handing me a glass of water.

"Thanks," I said, taking a seat. It was a hot July day and I drank the water in one long gulp. Placing the glass on the table I noticed a folded piece of paper partially concealed under a corner of the board. My heart stopped—*I recognized that slip of paper*. It was the one my father always carried in his breast pocket, close to his heart.

I glanced behind me, making sure the Old Arabs were sufficiently distracted by their dice-rolling, their shit-talking. Without waiting for my mind's blessing, my hand reached across the table and seized the slip from under the board. I unfolded it carefully like some ancient spiritual text, bracing myself for what it might reveal about the man I knew as my father.

In several lines, like a simple poem, it read: *paper towels, pistachios, pita bread, cigarettes.*

GOING THE DISTANCE: HOW COVID HAS REMAPPED FRIENDSHIPS

Sarmishta Subramanian

In the early days of the pandemic, a spate of stories appeared in the media proclaiming introverts the winners of the lockdown era. With a preference for small groups and time alone, the less outgoing among us seemed poised to thrive in this period. Introverts themselves embraced the idea. "With all this social distancing and takeout food, my life is about to dramatically stay the same," the comedian and satirist Randy Rainbow tweeted in mid-March last year. "Introverts: Flattening the curve since forever," quipped Jenn Granneman, an American who's spun her love of solitude into a profitable writing and blogging niche.

As a sometimes introvert, albeit a sociable one, I'll admit that in the early days it did seem as though the world had settled down to a velocity more in step with mine. The circumstances were grim. But public-health dictates meant no more dithering about dragging myself to a party, no pressure to make or keep dinner dates, no guilt about a weekend with zero plans. It was a silver lining in a dire time.

A year later, though, I find myself wondering if my introverted leanings did much to protect me. I'm not beset by anxiety or loneliness or melancholy; the feeling is both smaller

111

and bigger than that. Certainly, like many people, I've had moments of longing for a dinner out, coffee with a friend, a conversation with—god, anybody but these two lovely people in my home who never, ever seem to leave. But mostly I'm comfortable in my largely inward existence. Perhaps a little too comfortable. After a year of "stay home" and "stop the spread," that six feet of physical distance sometimes feels as though it has calcified into a shell.

I don't think I'm the only one. We are all introverts these days, and not by choice. So what happens as the virus recedes, and we look timidly toward reconnecting with our world? "After the Coronavirus, Prepare for the Roaring Twenties," read the title of an essay[1] by Yascha Mounk in *The Atlantic* last May, in the innocent days of the first wave. Mounk was weighing predictions, already proliferating, that our social natures will triumph post-pandemic—that once this is all over, we will go forth into a frenzy of socializing. More recently, the Yale sociologist Nicholas Christakis, author of *Apollo's Arrow: The Profound and Enduring Impact of Coronavirus on the Way We Live*, has looked to past pandemics to predict that people will "relentlessly seek out social interaction." There will be parties, carousing, an orgy of Sunday brunching and games nights (also, by some accounts, an orgy of actual orgies, but that is a topic for a different article by a different writer).

Will the prognosticators be right? It's possible. Around the time Mounk's article appeared, I spoke with a few psychologists about the effects of the pandemic on kids. Among them was Jean Twenge, a San Diego State University professor and bestselling author of books proclaiming various generational trends over two decades. Childhood the world over had, in a sense, moved online, and I wanted to know Twenge's thoughts on what this meant for young people, a group she dubbed "iGen" a few years earlier and believed was shaped by smartphones and screens to be more disengaged and lonely. I braced for a glum prediction. Her answer was more interesting. Sure, post-Covid, risk-averse young people hooked on social media could forgo real-world interactions even more, having fallen out of the habit, she said—or they might actually seek them out with a vengeance, having been denied that physical contact for so long. It could go either way.

I would think that forecast applies to the rest of us, too. I'd be surprised if many of us will want to stay in our respective bubbles after the pandemic. We have missed interacting with people. We've also learned in this time how much we need our friends, our extended families, the people in our wider circles. If the Covid era has shown with numbing efficiency the value of our most essential relationships, it has also revealed, through subtraction, the worth of those not deemed essential to daily life yet still vital to our happiness, our intellectual and emotional lives, our sense of who we are and can be. Many of us are determined, when normalcy returns, to make up for lost time. The question is what our relationships will look like after a year of enforced neglect and whether desire will translate to sustained connection. I don't doubt there will be parties. But will we remember how to be good social beings and fall back quickly into the give and take that meaningful human exchange demands? Or have we lost things to that six-foot gulf that has separated us for more than a year?

Twenty years ago, long before she became embroiled in campus wars over sexual relations and free speech, cultural critic Laura Kipnis published a provocative little book called *Against Love*. A polemic about the misery of romance, it detailed all the things domestic bliss forces us to give up. Here's a sampling from Kipnis's list, which will sound familiar to most people in a long-term relationship: You can't go out without telling the other person. You can't go out when your partner feels like staying at home. You can't do less than 50 percent of housework, even if your partner wants to do 100 percent more cleaning than you'd like. You can't watch what you want or eat what you want. You can't take risks, unless they are previously agreed-upon risks. "Thus is love obtained," Kipnis concludes wryly, putting the nail in the coffin of our forgotten freedoms.

Friendships don't make demands of nearly the same number or intensity. But there are still trade-offs for the companionship and intimacy they bring. If the friendship is healthy, neither person gets to do exactly what they want. Your friend doesn't eat gluten, so you go somewhere with options—even though you're really craving the carbonara from that Italian place. She's going through something at work, so you shut up about your life this time so she can tell you all about it (as in, all about it). You sit outside on the patio because she smokes; she accepts the reality that you will always be 10 minutes late. You put up with each other's quirks. I recall an evening spent at a friend's, a Nina Simone album playing on repeat on her stereo. We heard it four, maybe five times. I didn't say a word. She really liked Nina Simone, and I really liked her. Real human connection involves slightly uncomfortable states of perpetual compromise.

The logistics are in a sense ritual sacrifice, symbols of a deeper act of giving in, and letting in. Affairs of disentangled minds, as CS Lewis described friendship, come with both the risk and deep rewards of self-exposure. "Eros will have naked bodies;" Lewis wrote, "Friendship naked personalities." Could anything be more terrifying?

In the Before Times, I barely noticed these small acts of giving, big and small, let alone begrudged them. After a year of self-reliance, though, I wonder if my compromise muscle has atrophied, if I've grown so unaccustomed to negotiating those small things, so unused to the discomfort that can accompany vulnerability, that it will be harder for me to be a good friend when all this is over. Living with constraints may have diminished my tolerance for further constraint; my frustration threshold is lower than it used to be. And the rewards for those trade-offs—laughs, companionship, emotional intimacy—are such hazy memories now. I'd attributed these trepidations to my own introverted leanings, so I was surprised to hear an interview on NPR in which a California teacher, a self-described extrovert, related the changes she's observed in herself over months of social distancing. Before Covid, she said, she and her husband always had weekend plans: meeting friends, dinners out, movies. The pandemic has introduced her to the pleasures of alone time. Recently, she confessed, she found herself reacting with irritation to a distanced walk with a friend: "I felt like, oh, this is cutting into my normal routine. So it's very curmudgeonly."

Any event that casts others as intruders is not exactly a helpful influence in a society as individualistic as ours. Harvard political scientist Robert Putnam, in his 2000 book *Bowling Alone*, tracked the decline of social capital in America, evident in dropping rates of volunteering and participation in groups ranging from the B'nai Brith to the Girl Guides. Social media has made up for some of this loss of interaction. Still, a quarter of Canadians have fewer than three close friends, according to Statistics Canada data,[2] and in a 2019 Angus Reid survey,[3] six in ten wished their family and friends would spend more time with them. (We may be better off than our American neighbours, who have on average two confidants with whom they can discuss important issues, a 2011 Cornell University study found; one-quarter had none at all.)

Isolation is enough of a problem in the West that "social prescribing" programs began popping up in the UK in the 2010s, in which advisers work with GPs to prescribe patients community-based activities, such as cooking classes or karaoke. The Alliance for Healthier Communities has run a similar pilot program, called Rx: Community, in Ontario since 2018. For those who were already struggling with connection, the pandemic has only made things worse. The Covid-19 Social Study, conducted in the UK, surveyed 70,000 adults about how lonely they felt last year. As with social isolation pre-pandemic, those most affected by lockdown measures were people who are young (ages 18 to 30) or precariously employed, or live alone.

I am none of those things and would not have described myself as lonely before the pandemic. Yet a look at the questions was startling. The survey is very simple, with just three items: How often do you feel that you lack companionship? How often do you feel left out? How often do you feel isolated from others? I wonder how many of us, however gregarious we are, could honestly say "never" to all three.

It turns out that the whole introvert/extrovert distinction is less useful than it might seem. A 2020 Dutch study on depressive symptoms during Covid reviewed data from 93,125 subjects in 47 countries and found that introverts did fare better in places with more stringent pandemic measures, but that extroverts didn't necessarily suffer more. That's perhaps because of the nature of extroversion, which correlates with fewer anxiety and mental health issues. Introversion, a body of research shows, often comes with traits that help in adversity—the ability to reflect on experience, for one. But extroverts experience emotions less intensely and are more likely to show help-seeking behaviour, which is jargon for reaching out to a friend when you need one.

We are all muddling through it, then—sometimes awkwardly. I have noticed odd tics in my social habits. A friend came over for a backyard visit recently, and I greeted her with, well, no greeting at all, only a barrage of logistical options blasted out as I reached for a mask, just in case: "Do you want to sit on the front porch? Or shall we go to the back? Should I bring a blanket out? These chairs are far enough apart, right? Shall I make tea, or would you like sparkling water?" She answered my questions, and then paused. "Hi!" she said. "It's been so long!" It felt like the warmth of the sun. In our old life, she'd have come in. We'd have hugged. I might have said how long her hair was getting. They're just niceties, small ways of expressing a feeling that is much deeper and bigger—but without them, the feeling itself seems diminished.

The truth is, female friendships were besieged even before the pandemic. For so many women I know, those habits of connection—a phone call, a coffee date, regular dinner plans—were imperilled by the plague of busyness in professional and domestic life. Before the six-foot distance of the Covid era kept us apart, there was the 600-foot distance of work deadlines, kids' activities, eking out time with partners, running errands. Years ago, in my first journalism job, at *Chatelaine*, I coordinated a project to help the magazine's readers find close female friends they'd lost along the way, sometimes decades earlier. We ran a list in the magazine, and women saw their names on it and wrote in. Some of the letters were profoundly emotional, about living and loss and memories of girlfriends who got them through it. Female friendships can have that intensity. Mine certainly did; I was just out of university when we launched the project and couldn't fathom forgetting to stay in touch with my friends.

I've taken a master class in it since, as my friends apparently have too. I've had friendships fall into months-long, even years-long periods of benign neglect. We recovered, sometimes barely. But we had help: from coffee shops where we met, the chocolate-making or cookery classes we giggled our way through, the yarn store that in one phase of a particular friendship saw so many tears we feared for the fine mohairs and alpacas nearby, the offices in which some of us worked side by side. So much happens within six feet; proximity is, after all, why humans flock to the busy part of the dance floor or pack themselves into cities. To say nothing of the balm of human touch, the way a squeeze of an arm can comfort, soothe, dissipate a tense moment.

I don't know if that yarn store is still open, and coffee shops are little more than chilly lineups these days. (We'll leave the balm of human touch for a less blighted time.) Relationships lean on structures in ways we don't notice. The decline of work-friend routines, for one, is surely an under-acknowledged result of pandemic life. In an Australia–UK study on Covid's social impact, one in four adults ages 26 to 65 reported working fewer hours last year. We've read about the economic effects of reduced employment, but there's enormous social impact too. Think of all those so-called office marriages or the little gaggles of colleagues kvetching and chortling over coffee or a cafeteria lunch. What happened to those moments of friendship as people worked less or remotely or with the new constraints of masks and physical distancing?

We've lost ties not only to colleagues and friends but also to their friends, incidental social contacts that tether us to the wider village. Along the way we may have lost something unobserved: versions of our own selves—more gracious, charming, sparkling, *polite* iterations we inevitably reserve for those with whom we don't share our homes. The artifice demanded by less intimate friendships can be a marvellously beneficial force, smoothing our closest relationships and finessing the composite whole.

The pandemic has undeniably remapped friendships. Friend networks generally shrank in the past year, the data from open-ended questions asked through the Australia–UK project suggests. "When social interactions moved online, only certain kinds of relationships seemed to survive," Dr Marlee Bower, a loneliness researcher at the University of Sydney told the BBC. With lockdown measures in place, many of the social rituals of our lives disappeared: gym classes, after-work drinks, potluck dinners or girls' nights. The friendships that survived had to have some common ground besides shared interests or jobs. They also had to satisfy odd new requirements, like being tech-friendly or Covid-compatible.

I've seen my own social life reshaped by such vagaries. Friends I really like but who interpret public-health guidelines more loosely than I do fell off my social calendar (if it can be called that). The logistics just became too difficult. I know of friendships that have ended over pandemic-era travel or Covid vaccine hesitancy. I saw more of friends who occupied roughly the same segment of the happiness pyramid as I did because they were easier to be around than the ones exuberantly ticking every item off their pandemic bucket lists while I wilted. There are friends I hardly spoke with but remained intensely connected to, and others who seemed to vanish.

Some of the waning relationships were—unexpected bonus of pandemic life—replaced by friendships that intensified suddenly thanks to a shared world view that seemed all the more precious in this time. The clearing away of busy routines created the space for me to reconnect with a few neglected friendships. It rejuvenated my most local ones and (in snatches) some of my most distant ones—though I know that for some people, I was the friend who seemed to vanish. Physical distancing and guidelines to not mingle have sometimes brought more intimacy even while pushing some of us further apart.

Habits are strange creatures. There is no simple rule for breaking bad ones or making good ones, *The New Yorker*'s Charles Duhigg wrote in his book[4] on the subject. They operate on a complex system of cue and reward, and to change a habit, sometimes you must tweak one and sometimes the other—it is almost never simply a matter of willpower. If we have become habituated to being distant from people who matter to us but were for a year or more mandated to be inessential, we may struggle to build back our social habits when normal life returns.

But these are exceptional times, and I wonder if we can't trip the brain's circuitry into learning a new trick or improving on old ones. There were moments in the past year that reactivated mine: the walk through Toronto's Mount Pleasant cemetery on a frigid and windy December day that a friend took me on, pointing out Christmas arrangements and the statue of one particular angel I'd said my son liked—all via FaceTime, while I sat on my bed. The farmers'-market strawberries dropped off on my porch for no reason at all. The friend who sat on the phone with me for an hour on a glum July day and found my family a campsite so we had something to look forward to last summer. The surprise delivery for our annual Hannukah celebration with friends, by way of a computer this time. Minutes before the call, six exquisite and exuberantly flavoured doughnuts from across town arrived at my door. (My friend is vegan, and the doughnuts were too; I don't even want to think about what that cost.) And all those dumb little hearts and laughing-till-crying-face emojis and gossipy texts that travelled between my phone and my friends'.

A year of the pandemic has been brutal on many and not easy for even the luckiest of us. But even at a distance of six feet, there have been real moments of human communion. To thank the people who brought me some of those, I delivered a few items on March 13, the anniversary of the day the world shut down. My garbage collectors, mail-delivery person and local grocery workers got thank-you cards and cash. For my friends, who I knew would appreciate my streak of gallows humour unscathed by a global pandemic, I prepared cupcakes or cookies and homemade coronavirus-themed anniversary cards ("Happy Lockdown Anniversary!" or "Look who's one!"). The deliveries turned out to be an all-weekend affair, as my family and I stood on driveways and sidewalks around the city, chatting at a distance with friends we hadn't glimpsed in months. What half began as a gag turned into a deliberate act of friendship and care. It's the beginning, I hope, of new habits for a happier, sunnier time.

Notes

1 https://www.theatlantic.com/ideas/archive/2020/05/i-predict-your-predictions-are-wrong/611896/

2 https://www150.statcan.gc.ca/n1/pub/89-652-x/89-652-x2014006-eng.htm

3 https://angusreid.org/social-isolation-loneliness-canada/

4 *The Power of Habit: Why We Do What We do in Life and Business* (Anchor Canada, 2014)

ON AGEING ALONE

Sharon Butala

Although my memory of the details is vague, I think the following happened when I was eight years old, living in a village in central Saskatchewan and attending a one-room school with grades one through eight. Probably it was a hot day in June, we girls were wearing summer dresses, and because it was most likely a Friday afternoon, when everybody tends to slack off (or did in those days), our young teacher had sent us outside, around to the back of the school, to our baseball diamond. There, we were all—somehow, despite our being different ages, sizes, and genders—organized to play softball. I didn't enjoy sports, wasn't athletic, was a tiny child, and was bored. I remember standing in the batting lineup forever, as there was double the required number to a side, until finally it was my turn and I was berated by my teammates when I inevitably struck out. Because of all this, after a while, I wandered away from the game, around to the front of the empty school, and sat down, alone, on the wooden steps leading inside. Eventually, a sweating older girl came panting around the side of the building, looking for a drink of water. Seeing me, she hesitated and asked why I was sitting there by myself. I probably said that I didn't want to play ball—our mother didn't allow us to shrug our shoulders or say "I dunno" when she spoke to us, so I would have said something. She went on inside and at once came rushing back out, swiping water from her chin, and ran back to the game.

She must have told the teacher where I was. "Oh," the teacher must have said, and knowing I wouldn't be getting into mischief, seeing no other reason to insist I come back, the teacher left me there. This was just after the Second World War, when experienced teachers were in short supply. Ours was a teenager herself, with zero knowledge of child psychology, and she probably just couldn't be bothered. So I sat alone, listening to the crack of the bat on the ball and the cries of my classmates floating to me through the warm spring air over the roof of the school.

But, mostly, I remember sitting there, elbows on my knees, chin resting on my palms, and feeling . . . what? Peaceful and quiet, I think, aware of myself as alone in a wide noisy world yet enjoying my distance from it, if also feeling the creeping approach of loneliness. The boundary between solitude and loneliness is permeable and unstable, after all. I remember that, after a while, I got up off the steps and went back to the game. I remember that I found the teacher playing in the infield, sweat trickling down her temple, and when she glanced at me, her expression was somewhere between annoyed and indifferent. I already knew that look from my too-busy mother, who had five children under eleven to worry about, and I was by this time—at eight—girded against it.

Seventy years later, I still recall this moment, although without the shame I once associated with it—my peculiarities, my sullenness—as being when my status as a loner and a pursuer of solitude was cemented. Yet I and those friends my age who admit to suffering from loneliness do everything that remains within our power (not being able to bring the dead back to life or get rid of their own Parkinson's, arthritis, congestive heart failure) to relieve or dispel loneliness. I tell myself that everybody feels this emotion. It is some help but not much, and my inability to find the right or true source or cause of my loneliness is as painful as the loneliness itself.

When I was thirty-six, I left my lowly university-lecturer job in a small city to marry a cattle rancher whose land was in a sparsely populated and remote part of southwest Saskatchewan where, in time, I came to understand that I would never be fully accepted. Thirty-three years later, a widow dreaming of a new life (or to recreate my original one), I moved to Calgary to be near my grandchildren. Otherwise, I knew virtually no one there, and years later, my family gone to Ontario, I still don't have extensive or deep social connections. Ever since I left that remote Prairie home and chose the city, I have had the sense that my "real life," the place where I belong and where there is no loneliness, is somewhere else out there in the world, although I can't name or find it.

I'm eighty now and I live alone, a situation so common that you might even say loneliness goes hand in hand with being old, that the old are experts in loneliness. There is, however, a stigma attached to being lonely—being lonely must be your own fault because you're an inferior person—while, if you claim to enjoy solitude, you are seen as not of the typical run of humanity and are admired, even while being looked at skeptically, because in our society, preferring to be alone isn't seen as "normal" or well adjusted. Also, there is the tired disclaimer that you can be lonely while among people—and even in marriage—a cliché that, while true, only irritates those who are truly, physically alone in the world, such as orphans or the old whose family and friends are all too debilitated to connect with others or are dead.

We also all know, or at some juncture in our lives discover, that loneliness in North America is pervasive and thought to be caused by the cult of the individual, the nuclear family, the rise of narcissism, globalization, and late-stage capitalism. As

SHARON BUTALA

an old person, I live in the midst of a community of loneliness—admittedly a contradiction in terms: How do the lonely make a community and remain lonely? But, somehow, we manage it. The Covid-19 requirements of physical distancing and isolation have resulted in the sad, even alarming fact that loneliness is now more widespread through our society than it's ever been.

It is only when, having some long, heightened personal experience with loneliness, you decide to write an essay on this newly (again) trendy subject that you discover what a voluminous literature there is about it, from modern studies done by government departments to personal essays, from sixteenth-century Michel de Montaigne's "On Solitude" to psychiatrist Anthony Storr's 2005 *Solitude: A Return to the Self*. Both conclude that solitude is good while loneliness is bad and that loneliness is a complex emotion, state, condition. Put the topic in the hands of philosophers and you will soon find it is almost beyond your ability to understand their deep probing of the subject, examining related concepts of grief, sorrow, depression—even homesickness, although in old people homesickness is usually for the no longer extant home or for a home that, even if one went back and stood in the middle of it, wouldn't be the right, longed-for home anymore. And that would be loneliness. I am surprised to find that friends my own age who, before Covid-19, took part in the activities of a number of organizations so were out of their homes and with congenial people often—friends who never spent three to five days completely alone, the phone not even ringing unless it was the cursed telephone marketers—people who never used to go three to five days with no one knocking on the door and who didn't have to go to the grocery store or post office or even to the doctor just to have a human conversation, claim *still* to be lonely. How can this be?

We look back through our lives, thinking that loneliness didn't strike us at all when we were young, except—oh, yes—in certain, rare, specific situations: mom in the hospital, siblings gone somewhere without you, being sent off to the relatives while your parents holidayed, starting a new school, that kind of thing. Or, later, in adulthood: betrayal, divorce, living alone, changing cities, children leaving home, without the money to do whatever it is you want to do, dreaming of some life you can never have. Now, in old age, though, we are baffled by our loneliness no matter what we do to alleviate it; we resent it and start searching through the past to try to discover how we have come to this.

In a 2013 essay for *The New Republic* called "The Lethality of Loneliness," Judith Shulevitz writes, "Loneliness is made as well as given, and at a very early age. Deprive us of the attention of a loving, reliable parent, and, if nothing happens to make up for that lack, we'll tend toward loneliness for the rest of our lives. Not only that, but our loneliness will probably make us moody, self-doubting, angry, pessimistic, shy, and hypersensitive to criticism. Recently, it has become clear that some of these problems reflect how our brains are shaped from our first moments of life."

When I read this, I froze, so accurate a description it was of the tendencies that I fight in order to live a more "normal" life, of how I have gradually, over the many years of my adulthood, come to see myself as having been. That is, in order to not die of self-imposed loneliness. And, still, before Covid-19, I would catch myself dodging out of an event as soon as it ended, right when everybody else was gathering to network, bond, cement alliances, gossip, chat, and just have a little fun for half an hour before, satisfied, they would turn toward home. Or else I would refuse a social invitation because it intimidated me too much, even though everybody else would have a good time, and I probably would have too, if I could have just mustered the courage to initiate conversations or if I hadn't thought that the slightest, most fleeting expression meant the person I was talking to was bored by me or had taken a dislike to me. That

I had, once again, said something immeasurably stupid or offensive or had made an enemy when I was trying to make a friend. Rather than suffer through that again, I would tell myself, *I would rather be alone*. Even though Covid-19 has greatly exacerbated loneliness, I doubt, when it's over and I get used to going out again, I'll feel any different.

Not all the roots of loneliness grow from childhood. When I first became aware of myself as old, and when both of my parents, two of my four sisters, and my husband had died (the other two sisters, as well as my son and his family, live in other provinces, too far from me to visit casually even without Covid-19), leaving me pretty much permanently alone—in the physical sense, at the very least—I began to feel like the last member of my tribe left on earth. For the first time, I understood, in the deepest part of my being, what the true loneliness of orphans and of those who define themselves or are defined by society as "other," as not belonging, really is. I began to understand why the elderly are too often lonely people. But this is a kind of loneliness that is attached to being in the flesh, to once having been firmly related to others, to once having been a member of a large family or community. The soul remains connected to the dead, as if they were all still alive, but the body is bereft, and the mind rests in a kind of melancholy, awed confusion, and dismay. More than once, I have heard old people say, in a puzzled, sad way, something like, "I have outlived my life." I have said it myself. How can it be that I remain alive and on earth when the significant people of the life I have lived are now only ghosts? I have overstayed my life; my still being alive is a mistake; surely, I was meant to go when they did.

When I consider my own loneliness, now, in my old age, as I have done both on purpose and inadvertently, I count my blessings: a nice home; enough money to pay my bills; pretty good health for my age; a few good old friends in other provinces I can talk to on the phone; a few new friends with whom, before the virus and its isolation, I used to visit and with whom

I went to movies and plays; a brain that, though not as good as it once was, is still working well enough. This cures me for the moment, Covid-19 or not, but let my guard down and there it is again, like a mangy grey coyote that shadows me everywhere and that lay, forgotten by me, at my feet under the table when I was lunching with a friend, my loneliness problem solved until the moment the door latch clicked behind her and that coyote crawled out and rubbed against my leg once more. And I am baffled by this too, and thoroughly annoyed with myself because I knew—I know—better, if only I could remember what I know.

I was lonely after my husband died, in 2007, because I had no "significant other" reading the newspaper in the other room. But, as I adjusted to my single state, stifling that yearning, I turned to philosophers for instruction on the good life, the happy life, and in reading them, I suddenly remembered a teaching from many years ago, when I was wandering alone on the prairie one day, immensely sad, full of self-pity, and trying to understand where my dismal feelings came from.

There really was no one thing that I could pinpoint: I was sad because I was alive and did not have every single thing I had ever wanted, did not even know all the things I wanted, and I believe now that it was the latter that made me saddest. I was alive and I was a human being and wanting is the condition of the human. Words appeared in my head, or perhaps it was what I have called the "voiceless voice" that spoke to me. *This too is illusion*, it said, and at once, it straightened my head right around. Wisdom may sometimes come in such a flash, but I have learned you must stick with it or it will leave you as clueless as you were before it lit.

Loneliness isn't a social construct in itself, although social conditions can certainly create it: the loneliness of the prisoner, the loneliness of those doomed to live a life they think is not the one they would have chosen for themselves, the loneliness of the elderly caused by ageism. To suffer from loneliness is part of the human condition and must always have existed.

But it hasn't always been named as such. William Shakespeare, our greatest expert on everything human, left behind no indelible quotes about loneliness, as he did for just about every other human experience, despite being credited with coining the term "lonely." We, as readers, have never looked to him as someone who wrote about the subject. Was this because, for him, loneliness was fully tied to the condition of being unhappily in love? Or was it about the supposed loneliness of the dead? Nonetheless, Shakespeare's tragic heroes certainly suffered from what we would today simply call loneliness. King Lear, Hamlet, Timon of Athens, Coriolanus, and Titus Andronicus, in their extremities of rage, grief, and humiliation, were also lonely people.

Thomas Dumm, in *Loneliness as a Way of Life*, writes that "the very texture of modern life is inflected by loneliness." Thinking of the West, at least, who could disagree? Although Dumm, a professor of political science, goes on to write that loneliness permeates our entire experience of living and that it is also political because of the way it helps us understand and shape not just the meaning of our individuality but also how we use power and justice in the world. It is so ubiquitous an experience that, in January 2018, in response to a UK report finding that about 9 million people (out of 67 million surveyed) reported themselves as lonely and the fact that loneliness can be responsible for a decline in health, the British government appointed a so-called minister of loneliness. In late 2018, the government began serious work on a loneliness strategy, with the overarching department introducing a number of programs it believed would help alleviate the condition. (Currently, the "minister of loneliness" position no longer exists, though loneliness is the purview of the same department.) In February, alarmed by the increase in suicides it linked to the increased isolation of Covid-19, the

Japanese government also appointed a minister to oversee loneliness.

In Canada, governments are starting to pay attention to the problem and devise ways of alleviating it where they find it: chiefly, but not exclusively, among senior citizens. A good thing, because two Angus Reid Institute studies show that, in 2019, 55 percent of the population identified as having a good social life, but in 2020, the figure had dropped to 33 percent. The percentage of those reporting as not suffering from either loneliness or social isolation had dropped from 22 percent to 12 percent. But those suffering from both social isolation and loneliness (separated by the researchers, with sufferers of both referred to as "The Desolate") had increased from 23 percent to 33 percent. In 2020, one-third of our population was "desolate" from isolation and loneliness.

As if the simple continual longing for company isn't devastating enough, researchers have demonstrated that social isolation results in a weaker immune system, making the lonely more vulnerable to disease. A 2010 review of 148 studies on the health effects of social isolation found that they exceeded the health risks associated with obesity, inactivity, heavy drinking, air pollution, and smoking.

I have to question what agencies and programs designed to alleviate loneliness and instill a sense of community can do for the suffering. Besides offering transportation for people with disabilities and elderly people and language classes for non-English speakers, they can provide funding and leadership to create clubs and organizations designed especially for those groups defined as lonely. In some cases, all this may help quite a few people. But, in most of us, the fundamental condition will remain, even if at a diminished level, and for most of us, it ebbs and flows throughout our lives.

"We are all lonely, even when amid crowds and in committed relationships," writes psychoanalyst James Hollis in *Finding Meaning in the Second Half of Life: How to Finally,*

Really Grow Up. "When we are alone, we are still with someone; we are with ourselves. The question is how are we with ourselves?" Loneliness opens us up to self-questioning, sometimes to the obsessive mental repetition of past experiences and accompanying emotions, often to overpowering, helpless contrition for past deeds and words, to heightened mourning over our many losses, and to hopelessness. When you're alone, there is little to distract you from your thoughts, and if you have no one to talk to, your ideas about who you are and who you have been can ramp themselves up until rational perspective departs. Such suffering over your life can lead to despair. But Hollis writes that, if you have respect for yourself and if you pay attention to your dreams and "other such phenomena," you may find help with your loneliness from a deeper place within yourself. This is a psychoanalytic solution, deeply learned and intensely felt, and one that most people would be grateful for (and it will probably be as far as most of us get), but I think that, as helpful as such communing with the deeper self undeniably is, this response is still not quite the full answer to the problem of loneliness.

It shouldn't be forgotten that we are all afraid, even the greatest heroes and heroines among us. My own feeling is that perhaps the empty spot that pains us so deeply is, as I have written, yearning for what we have lost—our mother, spouse, child, original home, the way of life we left behind. "Our loneliness is always deepest in those moments when we face the terror of nothing," writes Dumm in *Loneliness as a Way of Life*. "But nothing rarely appears as itself; instead, it takes on many guises, most of which connect back to the ultimate nothing, death, or non-existence, that blank page."

And how do we deal with that? I think of myself as a person with a long history of being stifled by my own fears, and now, in old age, I think of the foolish ones: to drive in heavy traffic, to visit places where I know no one, to go out at night. I have wondered about them, berated myself over them, tried to overcome them, but I think I see now that, although there is much out there for old people to be afraid of, I suspect my fears are, in the end, related to my approaching nothingness—"that blank page."

One of the things that most puzzled me during the more than thirty years I spent with my husband in what was for me rural solitude—partly because I didn't fit into rural society and partly because I chose the work of learning to be a writer, which further isolated me—was that, even as I was often brought to an absolute physical halt by the natural beauty I was seeing, I was at the same time stricken painfully in the heart by the sight. Looking closer, I identified it as yearning, and then, in the end, I gave it the name of loneliness.

If I were more religious than I am, I might say that the feeling was yearning for the place we came from before we were born. But I don't quite believe that, although I would like to. Perhaps, instead, it is about the human search for perfection, the perfection we find only in great works of art and out in the landscape. I think that we yearn for perfect peace, which doesn't mean being in perfect solitude, or comatose, or brain dead, but for peace in the heart—a peaceful heart in the midst of the multitudes, tumult, chaos, violence, sorrow, and the beauty of everyday life. We can never have that peace, except in the work of art or the sunset, but instead, we have intimations of it, and that is why we feel sadness.

I have at times forgotten all about loneliness and, if asked, would have offered denial. My goodness, it's hard to be lonely in the middle of sex: the act occupies you rather fully, at least for a few minutes. And I wasn't lonely giving birth, although I was frightened, in pain, and perhaps indignant that this was bloody well asking too much of me. Or when I held my dearest preschooler tightly in my arms. Moments, flashes, the occasional long afternoon in the countryside, when dreaming, when lost in my work, in the "zone" athletes talk about, when struggling to understand an idea, whenever I am focused on something. Nor was I lonely when I was walking on the prairie alone and my consciousness moved out beyond its normal limits and allowed me a larger sense of the world.

It took nearly eighty years of living through happy things and sad things and torments of every kind that beset the human before I began to see how right the philosophers were: we are creatures of desire, creatures of the imagination, and to subdue these natural and vital processes takes a lifetime of repeated experience and the work that follows. No wonder wisdom suggests that we learn to focus on the now, forget the past, and stop worrying about the future. Only then does the sorrow vanish, only then do we erase loneliness. But, I think, at what great cost to the exploration of the richness of life and to individual human possibilities.

Still, sometimes I wonder how my life would have changed if, that day beside the school, my young teacher had come looking for me and, speaking to me encouragingly, had brought me to the others and ensured that I found a place in the game. Maybe I was waiting for her to do that, although I remember soon realizing that nobody would, one of the first revelations of my life. I was all alone, by my own not-exactly-choosing, since I wanted to be with the other kids but also wanted something else. Perhaps my need for solitude, despite its sometime companion loneliness, had been instilled in my soul long before I entered school, maybe at conception, and it would be up to me, as I grew, to find a balance where I could.

WE'RE ALL TEENAGERS NOW

Paul Howe

Most of us are familiar with the law of unintended consequences. In the 1920s, Prohibition put a halt to the legal production and sale of alcohol in the United States only to generate a new set of social ills connected to bootlegging and wider criminal activity. More recently, mainstream news media outlets, in pursuit of ratings and advertising dollars, lavished attention on an outlandish, orange-hued candidate when he first announced his run for president in 2015, and inadvertently helped to pave his way to the White House—oops. Aiding and abetting his campaign was a communications tool—social media—originally designed to bring people together and create community, but which now seems to serve more as a vehicle of division and discord.

A different development has been seen as an unqualified boon: the mass expansion, over the past century, of public education. In place of a small educated elite and the minimally schooled masses, we now have a society where the vast majority possess knowledge and skills necessary for success in various dimensions of their lives, including work, community engagement, democratic participation and more. Some might fall short of their potential, but the general impact is clear:

extending greater educational opportunity to one and all has provided untold benefits for both individuals and society at large over the long haul.

The latest work from Robert Putnam, the pre-eminent scholar of social change in the modern US, illustrates the common wisdom on the matter. His book *The Upswing* (co-authored with the social entrepreneur Shaylyn Romney Garrett) sets the stage by describing the social strife of the Gilded Age, the final decades of the nineteenth century when rapid industrialization and technological change generated social dislocation, inequality, civic discord and political corruption. In response to this troubled state of affairs, the Progressive movement sprang into being, bringing a new community spirit to society's problems, along with a series of pragmatic solutions. One signal achievement was the establishment of the modern public high school, an innovation that began in the US West and Midwest and spread quickly throughout the country. Enrolment at the secondary level among those aged 14 to 17 leapt from about 15 percent in 1910 to 70 percent by 1940.

In Putnam's account, the clearest benefit of educating Americans to a higher level was unparalleled economic growth and upward social mobility for the newly educated lower classes—positive effects that unfolded over the first half of the twentieth century and made the US a more prosperous and egalitarian society. These benefits were part and parcel of a more general upswing that encompassed rising levels of social trust, community engagement, political cooperation, and a stronger societal emphasis on "we" than "I."

But it did not last. For reasons not entirely clear, the 1960s saw individualism resurfacing as the dominant mindset of Americans and the ethos of US society, turning the upswing into a downswing that has continued to the present day and lies at the heart of many contemporary social and political problems.

Hidden in this puzzling arc of social change is another unintended consequence. Universal secondary education not only elevated Americans by spreading relevant knowledge and skills to the masses. It also gave rise to a more complex social and cultural transformation, as the adolescent period became pivotal in shaping who we are.

The fact is that high school is, and always has been, about more than just education. In the late 1950s, the sociologist James Coleman investigated student life in ten US high schools, seeking to learn more about adolescents and their orientation towards schooling. In *The Adolescent Society: The Social Life of the Teenager and Its Impact on Education* (1961), he reported that it was the social, not the educational, dimension of the high-school experience that was paramount to teens. Cloistered together in the high-school setting, teenagers occupied a separate and distinct social space largely immune from adult influence. Coleman warned that:

> The child of high-school age is "cut off" from the rest of society, forced inward toward his own age group, made to carry out his whole social life with others his own age. With his fellows, he comes to constitute a small society, one that has most of its important interactions *within* itself, and maintains only a few threads of connection with the outside adult society.

The emergence of a segregated teenage realm occurred well before Coleman put his finger on the problem. In their classic study of the mid-1920s, the sociologists Robert and Helen Lynd described the high school in "Middletown" (later revealed to be Muncie, Indiana) as "a fairly complete social cosmos in itself ... [a] city within a city [where] the social life of the intermediate generation centres ... taking over more and more of [their] waking life."

Life beyond the classroom reinforced the pattern: a national survey from around the same time found that the average urban teenager spent four to six nights a week socializing with peers rather than enjoying quiet nights at home with the family. With the advent of modern high school, the day-to-day life of teenagers was transformed, their coming-of-age experiences fundamentally altered. Adolescence became a kind of social crucible where teens were afforded the time and space to interact intensively with one another and develop by their own lights.

So while there was clear educational benefit gained from the reading, writing and arithmetic taking place in high-school classrooms across the land, a wider set of changes started to emanate from this new social configuration. The most visible was the emergence of a more sharply defined youth culture rooted in shared interests and passions that flourished more freely within adolescent society. Young people flocked to the movies like no other demographic, their enthusiasm for the silver screen and its celebrity icons helping to propel Hollywood to the forefront of popular culture. They latched on to new musical styles—jazz in the 1920s, swing in the 1930s—and embraced them as their own; devoured the new literary sensation of the times, comic books; and adopted common ways of dressing and personal styling as emblems of youth fashion. Embodied in these trends was a heightened emphasis on the fun and the frivolous side of life that would slowly reset societal standards as time went on.

Other changes were more subtle but equally portentous. Sociological studies conducted between the two world wars reveal a rapid liberalisation of attitudes towards practices such as betting, smoking and divorce, with rates of disapproval among youth declining by 20 to 35 percentage points in the space of just a single decade. In this same period, young people grew increasingly tolerant of social misdemeanours such as habitually failing to keep promises, using profane language, and keeping extra change mistakenly given by a store clerk—minor incivilities by today's standards, but harbingers of a changing social landscape where the transgression of established norms was starting to become more common and accepted.

This rapid evolution in everyday behaviour reflected a deeper transformation: the character of rising generations, their values, temperament and traits, were being reshaped by the powerful influence of peers during the formative years of adolescence. Hedonistic desires were more openly expressed, pleasurable activities more freely pursued. Conscientiousness was downplayed, social norms treated with greater scepticism and disdain. Impulsiveness and emotionality were more commonly displayed, an open, adventurous spirit widely embraced.

What these diverse adolescent qualities amounted to were the building blocks of a nascent individualism that would reshape society profoundly as they came to full fruition over the course of the next few decades. Traits conducive to self-focused and self-directed thought and action were more deeply etched in teenagers and slowly altered the character of society at large as whole groups socialized in this manner moved forward to adulthood.

The effects of peer influence, this argument implies, run deeper than is commonly imagined, affecting not just superficial features of the self during the teenage years, but the kind of person we become. Important research from the personality psychologist Judith Rich Harris, synthesised in her seminal book, *The Nurture Assumption* (1998), backs up this idea. Harris reviewed the body of research on the nature versus nurture debate, finding it consistently showed environmental effects outside the home loomed larger than had previously been realized. And she presented evidence that peers are among the most critical of these external influences on personality development. These scientific findings, applied to social history, help explain why the rise of universal secondary schooling was such a consequential development, as teen immersion in a society of adolescent peers became a critical facet of personal development and catalyst of social change from the early twentieth century onwards.

As time rolled on, further reinforcement and amplification of these effects came in the form of intergenerational abetting and encouragement. When the teenagers of the 1920s and '30s went on to have kids of their own in subsequent decades, they brought with them an adolescent-tinged perspective that influenced their own parenting practices, inclining them to give freer rein to their teenage offspring. The traits that parents (and indeed adults more generally) favoured in children shifted decisively over the long haul from obedience and propriety to independence and imagination, with the result that the expression and retention of adolescent qualities in postwar youth was stronger still.

That the spirit of the times was a-changin' became more obvious in the 1960s, when the youth cohort of that era expressed their adolescent rambunctiousness and exuberance with particular abandon and swerved even more strongly from "we" to "I" thinking: do your own thing, live and let live, anything goes. To most observers, then and now, it seemed like a dramatic turn of events, but the stage had been set by more subtle developments of the previous few decades that had seen successive generations of youth imbibing an individualistic mindset and manner from one another.

From this perspective, the 1960s looks more like a tipping point than a starting point: the moment when a process long on the runway took flight and suddenly became manifest to one and all.

Since then, the process has proceeded apace. Like earlier generations, the Baby Boomers of the 1960s retained much of their youthful orientation as they entered adulthood, losing the long hair and psychedelic attire, but retaining the mindset that had taken shape in their adolescent years. Slogans and behaviours that put "I" before "we" were absorbed into the wider culture, earning the 1970s the moniker of the "Me Decade."

New generations were thoroughly imbued, absorbing the prevailing cultural assumptions "like a fish accepts water," as the psychologist Jean Twenge put it in her book on the subject, *Generation Me* (2006). There are, of course, interesting debates around the distinctive character of more recent youth cohorts, including Millennials and Gen Z, groups known for their concern with the environment, social justice and human rights. Yet these recent shifts are relatively modest against the backdrop of a century of transformative social change.

As youthful ways of thinking and acting have slowly infiltrated adult society, we have arrived at a point where there is a much fainter demarcation line separating adults and teens. Film and TV have picked up on the theme in shows such as *Arrested Development* (2003–19) and movies starring Adam Sandler that depict immature adults set in their adolescent ways who are either unaware or unconcerned (perhaps both) about this state of affairs. In one episode of the TV show *Modern Family* (2009–20), Phil collaborates on a video with his son Luke that involves gamely taking dozens of basketballs to the head in the hopes that one will ricochet into the basket and produce an awesome clip. He grins at the camera as he reveals his motivation: "I've always said that if my son thinks of me as one of his idiot friends then I've succeeded as a dad." Yes, it's just TV, but it's funny because it has the ring of truth about it.

The real world is also replete with examples of adults acting like adolescents in many aspects of their lives. The phrase "unintended consequences" used at the beginning of this essay usually implies negative effects, but there are notable benefits as well. As a result of the gradual absorption of adolescent qualities, we've slowly chipped away at many rigidities of the adult world and grown more free-spirited, open and spontaneous—

sometimes even downright goofy, like the aforementioned dad from *Modern Family*.

These youthful character traits have served to make us more accepting and generous in many respects. Rising tolerance towards marginalized groups can be partly attributed to this emergent youthful mindset—a process normally seen as originating with the dynamic social movements of the 1960s and '70s, but which actually can be detected much earlier in the shifting attitudes of rising generations from the early twentieth century onwards. Traits connected to openness have also made us more creative compared with a century ago— contributing to the long-term rise of what the urban theorist Richard Florida has called the "creative class," people who value creativity and individuality in the workplace and other areas of their lives, and thereby contribute greatly to economic innovation and prosperity. The impact of adolescence on the adult world has played a major, and underappreciated, role in generating these vitally important liberating effects that have transformed life for the better over the long haul.

But there is an undeniable downside to the story as well. Many authors have traced the pernicious rise of impulsiveness, incivility and me-first brashness across different sectors of US life—social and cultural, economic and political. At the end of the 1970s, the historian Christopher Lasch wrote about a burgeoning "culture of narcissism," a concern echoed more recently by Twenge and W Keith Campbell in *The Narcissism Epidemic* (2010). The cultural theorist Paul Roberts focuses on the problems of instant gratification and consumerism run amok in *The Impulse Society* (2014), while the political scientist Alan Wolfe decries the political immaturity of the current age in *The Politics of Petulance* (2018). This is but a small selection of a wider literature of lament; the common thread, on my reading, is that many of these problems across different spheres of contemporary life can be linked to the excesses of youth that have been absorbed by the adult world.

The consequences connected to the more troubling aspects of our adolescent character seized public attention more fully once Donald Trump became president in 2016. If his political positions divided Americans, it was his manifest character defects that were most troubling to critics. It was no coincidence that many arrived at the same diagnosis, that Trump's instinctive reactions were more like those of a petulant child or angry teenager than a fully evolved adult. While such labels were sometimes applied for dramatic effect, professionals willing to venture an opinion generally agreed on the profound psychosocial shortcomings manifest in Trump's personality and behaviour.

The real problem, of course, is that he is not an isolated case. The tendencies Trump displayed—impulsiveness, belligerence, narcissism, a cavalier disregard for social norms—have grown all too common over time in society at large. One recent example is the stubborn refusal of many to wear masks during the Covid-19 pandemic, a political act on the surface, but at a deeper level a social phenomenon that could happen only in a society where many have lost touch with what it means to act like a mature adult in times of crisis and adversity. The larger social pattern helps explain how a man displaying symptoms of the same syndrome could gain the public support necessary to win the presidency once and nearly do it again.

While the Trump debacle rightly captured the world's attention and raised important questions about the dearth of adult qualities in US public life, the influence of adolescence on the adult world is not solely an American phenomenon. In other places where schooling through most of the teenage years has become the norm, the same process of social transformation has been initiated, reshaping societies in similar ways. Adolescent ways have seeped into adult society, upending traditional social norms and conceptions of adulthood. The effects have been broadly liberating, yet sometimes damaging, as the rise of adolescent-infused habits and assumptions has opened up avenues of behaviour that sometimes run counter to the common good.

But while the trajectory of social change is similar, there is one important difference: the US was first out of the gate as the forerunner in establishing a system of universal secondary education. The US high-school movement preceded all others, with the large majority of teens enrolled by the late 1930s, compared with a select minority—generally less than 25 percent—in other industrialised nations. Once secondary education was put in place, the transformative impact of adolescence was set in motion significantly earlier in the US than in other places.

Because of this, the US has advanced further down the road than most. It is in many ways the most adolescent of modern societies—a characterization suggesting a different spin on the notion of American exceptionalism, or perhaps more accurately, an additional layer. Yes, the US was different from the outset due to its foundational event, a revolution rejecting monarchy and colonial subjugation, and the explicit articulation of a freedom-focused public philosophy—life, liberty and the pursuit of happiness. But the precise meaning and implications of that phrase are ambiguous and can take a country in many different directions depending on how it is interpreted and applied. Over the past century, the words have been infused, and the society imbued, with values reflecting the instincts and sensibilities of the young. The founding philosophy and adolescent ethos together have proven a potent combination, guiding the US towards an immoderate individualism—*my* life, *my* liberty, the pursuit of *my* personal happiness—that contributes greatly to many current-day social and political problems.

Progressive reformers had the best of intentions when they provided secondary schooling for one and all. But that educational project helped trigger a parallel social transformation that has undermined at least some of their good work. After a century, the world of adolescents has given rise to a world of adolescence. It is important to examine social history closely, and to unpack the deep sources of current problems, if we hope to set some of this straight and make the US—and the world—a better place.

Parts of this essay are adapted from Teen Spirit: How Adolescence Transformed the Adult World *(2020) by Paul Howe, published by Cornell University Press.*

RESCUING THE RADICALIZED DISCOURSE ON SEX AND GENDER

Part Two of a Three-Part Series

Allan Stratton

Our choice of words affects the way we think. That's why we spend so much time fighting over which terms to use, whether it's "undocumented immigrants" versus "illegal aliens," "foetuses" versus "unborn babies," or "militants" versus "terrorists." In recent years, the question of word choice has figured prominently in the activism of gender supremacists (as I described them in the first entry in this essay series), who seek to entirely replace biological sex with self-identified gender as a legal category.

According to the Catholic doctrine of transubstantiation, a priest's blessing transforms the material substance of communion wafers and wine into the actual body and blood of Christ, even as the wafers and wine retain their outward appearance. Gender supremacists have a comparable doctrine—let's call it transgenderation—by which the faithful must believe, literally, that "transwomen are women."[1] (It also demands that transmen are men, though it's interesting to observe that the male-identified half of the trans community isn't nearly so strident in its insistence on transgenderation as the female component.) I am not speaking figuratively here: A leading trans scholar at Berkeley, Grace Lavery, has claimed[2] that (in the words of the university's own headline writers[3]) "truly changing sex is possible."

As someone who has lived the internal politics of the LGBT community for decades (being of the G persuasion), I've noted that many of the gender-supremacist movement's most doctrinaire high priests are trans women who, notwithstanding their loud and proud self-identification, seem quite happy with their penises and chest hair. Their internet acolytes typically consist of mostly straight, bi, or queer-identified young people who are eager to sign on to what seems like a progressive movement. The priests aren't elected, nor do they seem to represent the bulk of transgender individuals (who generally have a more realistic understanding of how biology works). However, the priests have been able to maintain their influence, and protect themselves from criticism, through word games and the threat of quick-trigger transphobia accusations.

But you don't have to understand Catholic doctrine to know how this game works. The Looking-Glass world of Lewis Carroll is good enough:

> "When *I* use a word," Humpty Dumpty said, in rather a scornful tone, "it means just what I choose it to mean—neither more nor less."
>
> "The question is," said Alice, "whether you *can* make words mean so many different things."
>
> "The question is," said Humpty Dumpty, "which is to be master—that's all."

Humpty Dumpty's will to power is instructive here, because the public discussion about trans rights, in most cases, is no longer about being kind and respectful toward trans people—a principle that everyone of goodwill now generally agrees on. Rather, it's a project aimed at manipulating language as a means toward mastery in areas of policymaking where the rights of transwomen (in particular) conflict with other rights, including those of women who seek to keep their intimate spaces[4] free of male-bodied individuals, and parents who feel that their children are being pressured[5] to use transition as a means to deal with unrelated traumas or psychological conditions.

The word we once used to describe the men (as most of them were) who experienced gender dysphoria was transsexual. And while transsexual individuals were obviously part of the LGBT community in earlier eras, they were a small part, as the (physical) barriers to entry were considerable, and trans status wasn't thought to be based on a simple act of self-declaration. (The Amsterdam Gender Dysphoria clinic, which has treated the vast majority of Dutch transsexuals for decades, reports that physically transitioned transsexual women account for only about one in 10,000 men, and physically transitioned transsexual men account for only about one in 30,000 women.)

In 1991, German sexologist Volkmar Sigusch created terminology to describe the 99.9+ percent of men and women who were comfortable with their birth sex: "cis" or "cissexual" (*zissexuell* in the original German). Since then, "cis" has migrated from a description of sex, and now is more commonly used to describe internally felt gender identity. Indeed, it is now routine for progressive educators to instruct children that they may be cis or trans in the same way that they may be gay or straight.

Since cis and trans are presented as adjectives, they apply equally to the nouns they modify—much like tall or short, heavy or thin. Thus, a man can be a man with a penis, or a man with a vagina, just so long as you put the right syllable ("cis" or "trans") in front of the word "man." This linguistic transformation has altered the meaning of words such as "man" and "woman" in a way that the adjectives "gay" and "straight" never did. It also allows radical gender activists such as ACLU lawyer Chase Strangio to emit such mantras as "Women and girls[6] who are trans are biological women and girls." As Humpty Dumpty might explain to a confused Alice: since genitals are irrelevant, and everyone has a biology, transwomen *must* be biological women.

A related consequence is that the term "birth sex" now has no meaning. That's why it's currently being replaced by the awkward "sex *assigned* at birth." After all, if boys and girls aren't identified by their penises and vaginas, we can't say what they are until they tell us. (The term originally was used to describe babies with actual intersex[7] conditions, who account for only a tiny percentage of births.)

These word games are politically useful: If the sex binary doesn't exist, not only are the terms "man" and "woman" de-sexed, but the concept of *transsexualism* disappears as well. This is handy for the self-described transwomen who don't actually suffer any kind of gender dysphoria (i.e., unease at a mismatch between sex and gender identity)—a male-bodied constituency that accounts for much of the activism in this area. After all, if bodies don't matter, neither do the sex reassignment surgeries that draw attention to the definitional importance of male and female body parts. This explains, among other things, why transsexuals who continue to define themselves as such are seen as collateral damage to the gender-supremacist cause.

What we are left with is an imposed system of language that has no connection to physical reality, or to the "lived experience" of anyone except the tiny subset of a subset that created it. In Orwellian fashion, these activists have locked in their favoured dogma by defining the applicable terminology in such a way that dissent is rendered impossible.

This lurch into the Looking-Glass world is presented as the height of progressive enlightenment. But it's the opposite: For over 60 years, I watched the LGBT and women's movements separate the concepts of sex and gender, so that effeminate boys ("genderqueer" or "gender non-conforming," in modern parlance) could grow up to be Quentin Crisp,[8] and girls could be Fran Liebowitz,[9] all without judgment and harassment. The more avant-garde approach, on the other hand, erases the real distinction between sex and gender by demanding that the former be subordinate to the latter. But of course, gays, lesbians, and bisexuals experience same-*sex* attraction on the basis of real biological sex, not the abstraction of gender.

That attraction is foundational to our lives and self-understanding. Yet it is systematically denied by gender supremacists, who are incapable of reconciling their claims about human identity except through the fiction that humans are sexually attracted based on the gender self-identification of potential partners. (To give up this claim would be to admit that a lesbian isn't going to be attracted to a male body, no matter how many times she is assured that the body in question belongs to someone who identifies as a woman.) The LGB population, in other words, has effectively been gaslit to fit the ideological convenience of a subset of trans activists—a deeply homophobic project.

Far from speaking for the entire LGBT community, gender supremacists don't even speak for many trans people. They certainly don't speak for trans pioneers such as cross-dresser Virginia Prince[10] (a self-identified heterosexual man), or drag kings and queens such as Stormé DeLarverie,[11] who realized that their creative and non-traditional ideas about gender didn't alter their underlying sex. Nor do gender supremacists speak for trans heroes such as Aimee Stephens[12], a Michigan funeral director whose case went to the US Supreme Court[13]. Stephens had been fired by her employer precisely because her gender identity didn't align with her actual sex. (The funeral home allowed women to wear skirts, but refused Stephens's request to do so on the basis of her male biology. In other words, *sex* discrimination was at the centre of the case and the basis of her victory.)

Nor do gender supremacists speak for transsexuals such as veteran activist Buck Angel[14], who self-describes[15] as "born biologically female." ("I use testosterone to masculinize myself so I feel more like me," he has written on Twitter. "I had a legal sex change and now live as a male. All male pronouns. I am a transsexual and will never be biologically male. But I do live as a male.")

"The whole point to my transition was to be seen as a male, live as a male, but to always be honest about where I came from," Buck told me. "I'm a biological female and that truth is what this new ideology is trying to eliminate, along with the understanding of dysphoria. To say you are a non-dysphoric trans person makes zero sense. It's very insulting to the people who actually struggle with gender dysphoria. We're getting bashed by this new ideology. Not sure how can they come in and completely coopt our identity, then act all insane when we fight to keep it."

Debbie Hayton, a trans British high school physics teacher, also has taken a public stand for the reality of biology[16]. "Transsexualism is a response to a psychological condition, and transition is something we did to improve our mental health," she argues. "We're trans because we *did* something. Our response and experience are being used by others to 'validate' their identities, whatever that means. This frustrates me, because while I can make the distinction between transsexual and transgender others don't."

Kay Brown is a transsexual activist who transitioned to a female identity four decades ago,[17] and the author of a must-read article[18] entitled "How the Big Tent Transgender Movement Distorts Science and Holds Back Civil Rights for Transsexuals." She says that even the very word she uses to describe herself, "transsexual," is now employed as a term of abuse[19] by self-described transgender activists who (unlike Angel, Hayton, and Brown) don't actually experience clinical gender dysphoria. She also describes being dismissed as "truscum" (which Urban Dictionary defines[20] as "A queer individual [who] holds the belief that you require gender dysphoria to identify as transgender").

Brown equally dislikes being misidentified as transgender. "The first time I got called 'transgender' by a doctor, in 1996, I almost bit his head off," she says. "I wanted to *scream*. Up to the 1990s, transgender meant straight men who role-played as 'girls' on 'girls night out' at the local gay bar mid-week when [business] was slow enough that the management tolerated their presence. Two transsexual friends mistakenly went to such an event. 'Close your eyes. What do you hear?' 'A bunch of straight men talking loudly.' 'Right, we don't belong here. Let's go.'"

Trans people deserve to be able to self-identify and self-understand as they wish. But everyone else has the *same* right—including women who lack the privilege or entitlement to trivialize their sex as a badge of identity. Their self-understanding as women is centred on the biological urgency of pregnancy, miscarriage, childbirth, menstruation, and menopause; and (even if they go through life without experiencing some or all of these events) bodies that are evolutionarily programmed to accommodate these processes. Their fight for the right to vote, work, drive, enter into contracts, and control their own bodies emerged from this reality, which also has included such sex-specific horrors as genital circumcision, sex slavery, menstrual huts,[21] rape, honour killings, and live burial and burning upon widowhood. The refusal of gender supremacists to allow women the language of their bodies and historical experience is brutal. It is also deeply hypocritical, given the emphasis trans activists typically place on the idea that language can serve to oppress or even "erase" someone.

A woman working within the medical bureaucracy here in Canada reports to me: "When I'm working on perinatal guidelines, I'm told that the word 'woman' isn't safe for trans people. We're told to use 'chest feeding' and 'pregnant individual,' never breast or women. I think we should be gender inclusive rather than gender neutral. Transmen are maybe .001 percent of people who give birth. We should be welcoming, but we shouldn't direct all our energies to *their* issues and away from the issues that affect *women* giving birth."

It may be tempting to dismiss this as mere political correctness—a harmless attempt to err on the side of sensitivity. But these linguistic choices reflect the very real demands of trans activists to pretend away the biologically rooted differences between men and women.

Influential American trans polemicist Julia Serano, for instance, seems genuinely mystified, and even angry, at the lesbians who reject her male genitals[22] as an object of sexual attraction. "If it were only a small percentage of cis dykes who were not interested in trans women at all, I would write it off as simply a matter of personal preference," she wrote in 2017. "But this is not a minor problem—it is systemic; it is a predominant sentiment in queer women's communities. And when the overwhelming majority of cis dykes date and fuck cis women, but are not open to, or are even turned off by, the idea of dating or fucking trans women, how is that not transphobic?" (For the record, Serano is also upset at trans men with vaginas: "Trans male/masculine folks who claim a place in dyke spaces by emphasizing their lack of male genitals or their assigned-female-at-birth status royally screw over their trans sisters.")

"There's a real lack of kindness and empathy about what we go through as lesbians," a friend of mine told me. Like the woman working in a hospital, quoted above, and almost every other "cis" woman I've interviewed on this subject, she asked for anonymity. They now operate under the fear that stating certain obvious facts—for instance, that lesbians are attracted to vaginas and breasts, not penises—will lead to being mobbed on social media and possibly even fired from their jobs.

The idea of "safety" is never far from the surface in these discussions—a common feature of moral panics, which always are animated by the belief that heterodox opinions could endanger human life. "Public safety" was behind the puritanical laws that kept gays and lesbians in the closet. For LGBT organizations to weaponize this kind of rhetoric today is an insult to the community they serve. It also makes us look ignorant and oversensitive, given that LGBT communities in other parts of the world are fighting for basic rights in the face of state-sponsored torture and killing, and so don't have the luxury of complaining about not being lusted after by, as Serano puts it, "cis dykes" or their male equivalents.

As an adult, I discovered that 10 percent of my high school and university residence friends were gay. Each of us thought we were alone because we were afraid to reach out. I see parallels when it comes to today's intellectual closet: People are afraid to say what they think, even when it comes to obvious facts concerning their own biological makeup and sexuality.

At the same time, many of the loudest voices in the LGBT activist (and "allyship") community are only nominally queer, their ranks being padded with legions of allegedly bi women and their boyfriends, who simply role-play, experiment, fantasize beyond the vanilla, and grab attention by writing about their queer haircuts.[23] Now a casually assumed identity, "Queer" once was the gay N-word—the last word many gay men heard as they were beaten and killed. Many of us reclaimed it during the AIDS pandemic—"We're here, we're queer, get used to it"—and then continued to use it as a synonym for gay (especially when discussing our community in a political context). Its increasingly watered-down usage by bourgeois dilettantes represents an offensive trivialization of our history.

In 1999, Kimberly Peirce directed the ground-breaking film *Boys Don't Cry*,[24] which, for the first time, brought the issue of anti-trans violence to a mainstream audience. Even today, studios rarely back female directors. Back then, Peirce's path was even harder—especially given her identity as a non-binary lesbian who wanted to make a movie about people whom many people considered freaks. But after years of effort,

Peirce's dedication paid off. Her film won a slew of awards and attracted widespread support to the trans cause.

In 2016, however, queers at Reed College in (where else) Portland tore into her at a campus presentation. Why? Because she'd cast the non-trans actress Hilary Swank as pre-op Brandon Teena. Placards read: "Fuck Your Transphobia!," "Fuck this cis white bitch," and "Fuck you scared bitch." Some arts journalists[25] even cheered them on, arguing that change was needed so that "transgender people won't feel their *only* recourse is to label a celebrated queer filmmaker as a bitch" (*my italics*).

Or consider Martina Navratilova, one of history's great tennis stars, who lost millions in endorsements[26] as an out lesbian in the 1980s. A lifelong campaigner for equal rights, her trainer was trans pioneer Renée Richards.[27] But when a late-transitioning Canadian trans academic then going by the name of Rachel McKinnon (since rebranded as "Veronica Ivy") began winning women's cycling races a few years back, Navratilova tweeted[28]: "You can't just proclaim yourself as female and be able to compete against women." She clarified in the *Times*[29]: "I am happy to address a transgender woman in whatever form she prefers, but I would not be happy to compete against her. It would not be fair." Twitter went full Inquisition, and Navratilova was blackballed[30] as a bigot by the LBGT charities she'd worked for, a humiliation broadcast in the mainstream press and now the only safe opinion on progressive social media.

We now live in a world where even RuPaul—drag's grande dame since the 1990s, who made drag mainstream through *RuPaul's Drag Race*—can be denounced as a reactionary. In 2018, RuPaul noted that drag's power is based on the inversion of sex roles, and "loses its sense of danger[31] and its sense of irony once it's not men doing it, because at its core it's a social statement and a big F-you to male-dominated culture." This is why, RuPaul explained, he never cast trans women as drag queens. "You can identify as a woman and say you're transitioning, but it changes once you start changing your body.

It takes on a different thing; it changes the whole concept of what we're doing."

RuPaul was denounced[32] by twenty-somethings as a transphobe[33] who didn't understand drag.[34] He responded like any great queen: "You can take performance-enhancing drugs and still be an athlete, just not at the Olympics." The response was consistent with his unapologetic stance during an earlier controversy, when he'd brushed off activists' complaints about his gender-bending wordplay[35]: "We take feelings seriously and intention seriously, [but] if you are trigger-happy[36] and looking for a reason to reinforce your own victimhood, your own perception of yourself as a victim, you'll look for anything that will reinforce that." By 2018, however, offending the trans lobby had become more radioactive. Facing brand meltdown, RuPaul apologized, and called his critics "my teachers."

In Canada, they came for Sky Gilbert, co-founder and artistic director of Buddies and Bad Times Theatre,[37] the largest LGBT theatre in North America during the 1980s and 1990s. As he described[38] to *Quillette* readers in 2019, the company had planned a staged reading of his 1986 hit play *Drag Queens in Outer Space* as part of its 40th anniversary celebrations. But when self-described *Trauma Clown*[39] Vivek Shraya attacked gay men in her 2018 book *I'm Afraid of Men*,[40] Gilbert wrote a response on his blog, which he titled "I'm Afraid of Woke People."[41] Shraya herself had no comment, but queer heresy-hunters accused Gilbert of racist violence against the trans community. Buddies denounced[42] him, and replaced the reading with a three-and-a-half hour struggle session.[43] So it came to pass that Sky Gilbert, who fought for minorities and hired trans folk before Shraya was born, became *persona non grata* at the company he'd founded.

Woke doctrine holds that the feelings of individuals from marginalized groups should act as a checkmate on further discussion, lest they suffer trauma or emotionally experienced "violence." But *whose* feelings count within these groups?

Peirce is a butch lesbian who broke pink and glass ceilings. RuPaul is a gay Black kid who overcame poverty, sexual trauma, and drug abuse. Navratilova is an immigrant lesbian. Gilbert is a drag queen.

Perhaps nowhere is the totalitarian push to silence dissent on the subject of gender more evident than in the campaign to demonize lifelong LGBT ally and advocate JK Rowling as a transphobe. The mobbing began in earnest in 2019 after Rowling tweeted[44]: "Dress however you please. Call yourself whatever you like. Sleep with any consenting adult who'll have you. Live your best life in peace and security. But force women out of their jobs for stating that sex is real?" She was referring to Maya Forstater, a British woman who'd lost her job for tweeting that, owing to biology, she believed trans women were men.[45] Forstater had appealed to an employment tribunal, and a judge had ruled against her. (That judgment, in turn, was overturned[46] by a High Court in a decision that tore the tribunal judgment to shreds.)

In a subsequent essay,[47] Rowling underlined both her support for trans women, but also her support for women's sex-based privacy rights, speaking as the survivor of a violent sexual attack. She explained, "I believe the majority of trans-identified people not only pose zero threat to others, but are vulnerable for all the reasons I've outlined. Trans people need and deserve protection . . . I want trans women to be safe. At the same time, I do not want to make natal girls and women less safe. When you throw open the doors of bathrooms and changing rooms to any man who believes or feels he's a woman—and, as I've said, gender-confirmation certificates may now be granted without any need for surgery or hormones—then you open the door to any and all men who wish to come inside. That is the simple truth."

The detail that many critics missed (or claimed to miss) was that Rowling wasn't speaking about any danger from trans women. Rather, she was discussing the danger that the policy of unfettered self-identification poses to women, insofar as it may be taken advantage of by predatory men *posing* as trans. People (of all types) have assumed false identities since Jacob tricked Isaac[48] and Odysseus returned to Ithaca disguised as a wandering beggar. Every week, another case of race-shifting[49] is exposed. Why should gender self-identification be uniquely free of grift?

Yet two years later, hatred of Rowling remains *de rigueur* in progressive LGBT circles. Eddie Izzard, the once-transvestite comic, was cheered in December[50] when she came out as trans with she/her pronouns. But baby queers told her to "do better"[51] in January when she came to Rowling's defense, notwithstanding that Izzard was already wearing frocks when their parents were in grade school.

The point at which the trans activist cause became so radicalized that it put itself in opposition to feminism and gay rights is hard to identify with precision. But according to Hayton, it was when mere self-identification was taken as the gold standard of who was a man and who was a woman—a policy that's become encoded in law in many jurisdictions over the last decade. Once that proposition was embraced, all of the other outrages followed: biological men competing in women's sports, violent male criminals suddenly self-identifying as women so they can do their time in female prisons, and fully intact men proudly taking photos of themselves in women's bathrooms. "There was widespread acceptance of transsexuals in women's spaces when I transitioned in 2012," says Hayton. "But the assumption was that you'd changed your body or were going to, and this was a response to a medical condition. Moving it from a medical to a social issue has damaged our acceptance. If pre-op trans women are let in, how do you stop any male person who claims to be some sort of woman?"

There is much basis for solidarity among gays, lesbians, and trans people. Decades ago, we were the ones being subject to psychiatric evaluations, and stigmatized with the label of mental illness. We, too, were accused of being sexual predators who could not be trusted in washrooms (and may other places besides). But we met the charges honestly, not by tricks of language or countervailing hate campaigns against our critics.

When today's gender priesthood refuses to engage even good-faith LGBT allies, they abdicate the moral high ground and lose all credibility. Unable to persuade, they resort to bullying. Such aggressive tactics have allowed them short-term success in academia, arts, government, and NGO circles, where employees and administrators fear the professional consequences that go with ideological heterodoxy. But this success has come at a price, as there is now a large and growing group of disaffected progressives, LGB and otherwise, who see militant trans activists not as allies, but as political liabilities who have hurt our cause—right down to the language we use to describe our very being.

Notes

1   https://abigailshrier.substack.com/p/transwomen-are-women-and-other-polite?s=r

2   https://financialpost.com/opinion/junk-science-week-this-just-in-biological-sex-is-a-myth

3   https://news.berkeley.edu/2021/06/14/qa-with-grace-lavery/

4   https://www.instagram.com/p/CQgfGijHyrv/

5   https://quillette.com/tag/when-sons-become-daughters/

6   https://twitter.com/cityoftoronto/status/1385950823503613952

7   https://quillette.com/2020/06/07/jk-rowling-is-right-sex-is-real-and-it-is-not-a-spectrum/

8   https://www.youtube.com/watch?v=34GW5edcyy4

9   https://www.youtube.com/watch?v=Hkc71hM9vT0

10   https://www.uvic.ca/transgenderarchives/collections/
     virgina-prince/index.php

11   https://www.gq.com/story/storme-delarverie-suiting

12   https://www.cnn.com/2020/06/15/politics/aimee-stephens-
     scotus-ruling/index.html

13   https://www.cnn.com/2020/06/15/politics/supreme-court-
     lgbtq-employment-case/index.html

14   https://twitter.com/buckangel

15   https://twitter.com/BuckAngel/
     status/1209236297140834304

16   https://quillette.com/2020/02/02/i-may-have-gender-
     dysphoria-but-i-still-prefer-to-base-my-life-on-biology-
     not-fantasy/

17   https://sillyolme.wordpress.com/

18   https://sillyolme.wordpress.com/2017/04/16/getting-lost-
     in-the-crowd/

19   https://twitter.com/Display_Geek/
     status/1171956416027848704

20   https://www.urbandictionary.com/define.
     php?term=truscum

21   https://www.bmj.com/content/368/bmj.m536

22   https://www.thedailybeast.com/the-struggle-to-find-trans-
     love-in-san-francisco

23   https://xtramagazine.com/love-sex/queer-haircut-straight-
     boyfriend-197564

24   https://www.imdb.com/title/tt0171804/

25   https://www.indiewire.com/2016/12/kimberly-peirce-boys-
     dont-cry-reed-transgender-1201757549/

26   https://theintercept.com/2020/07/14/cancel-culture-
     martina-navratilova-documentary/

27 https://www.tennis.com/news/articles/decades-later-renee-richards-breakthrough-is-as-important-as-ever

28 https://bleacherreport.com/articles/2821380-martina-navratilova-transgender-athletes-in-womens-sport-is-insane-cheating

29 https://www.thetimes.co.uk/article/the-rules-on-trans-athletes-reward-cheats-and-punish-the-innocent-klsrq6h3x

30 https://edition.cnn.com/2019/02/20/tennis/martina-navratilova-dropped-lgbt-group-scli-spt-intl/index.html

31 https://www.theguardian.com/tv-and-radio/2018/mar/03/rupaul-drag-race-big-f-you-to-male-dominated-culture

32 https://www.independent.co.uk/voices/rupaul-drag-race-transgender-guardian-interview-gender-identity-patriarchy-a8239041.html

33 https://www.dailyuw.com/opinion/article_945fbd6c-9b0a-11ea-81db-ff871a85f1cc.html

34 https://www.youtube.com/watch?v=-y00mvRA9xs

35 https://www.vox.com/culture/2018/3/6/17085244/rupaul-trans-women-drag-queens-interview-controversy

36 Ibidv/

37 https://www.canadiantheatre.com/dict.pl?term=Buddies%20in%20Bad%20Times

38 https://quillette.com/2019/06/01/watching-my-own-excommunication-on-a-facebook-video/

39 https://scotiabankcontactphoto.com/archive/2019/trauma-clown-2/

40 https://www.penguinrandomhouse.ca/campaign/665/im-afraid-men

41 http://skygilbert.blogspot.com/2018/11/im-afraid-of-woke-people.html

42 https://nowtoronto.com/culture/stage/buddies-in-bad-times-sky-gilbert-long-table

43 https://www.facebook.com/watch/live/?v=922888617920697&ref=watch_permalink

44 https://twitter.com/jk_rowling/status/1207646162813100033?lang=en

45 https://www.bbc.com/news/uk-50858919

46 https://www.bbc.com/news/uk-57426579

47 https://www.jkrowling.com/opinions/j-k-rowling-writes-about-her-reasons-for-speaking-out-on-sex-and-gender-issues/

48 https://www.biblegateway.com/passage/?search=Genesis%2027&version=NCV

49 https://www.insidehighered.com/news/2021/06/15/allegations-playing-being-indigenous-queens-u

50 https://www.advocate.com/transgender/2020/12/21/eddie-izzard-girl-mode-says-pronouns-are-shehers

51 https://www.themarysue.com/eddie-izzard-defending-jk-rowling-not-the-energy-we-need/

52 https://www.instagram.com/p/CQgfGijHyrv/

AFGHANISTAN, THE BEAUTIFUL LAND OF ENDLESS SUFFERING

Jamaluddin Aram

> *Padshah Gardeshi: A Dari phrase for when a king is dethroned. It has also come to mean when a government is toppled and replaced by a new one. The latest happened on Sunday, August 15, 2021. Taliban ousted President Ashraf Ghani who fled to United Arab Emirates.*

My grandfather died never having known when he was born. I think he didn't care about the beginning of something he could already see the end of, especially from where he lay in the hospital bed with the scars in his liver, and the clear tube carrying the greenish fluid from his swollen belly down into a large pail on the floor. I can still taste the salt and metal in the vapor from the pail in the cold room, and remember the snow falling outside and the calm on my grandfather's ashen face. He knew then what I know now: that the key to life is to have no expectations, to know what to remember and what to forget, and to have patience. A good amount of the latter if your motherland is called Afghanistan. You would need it.

Like my grandfather, I don't know my birth date and I don't care either. I was born on some grey winter day around the time the last Red Army soldier crossed the Friendship Bridge.

"It was cold and rainy," my mother says, looking out the window, her eyes bright with remembering. "At the time of the Saur Revolution, your sister was four years old," she continues. When that cholera plague swept through town, it took Aunt Diljan with it, but she returned from the edge of death, having no recollection of the horror she had suffered. This, my mother doesn't have to say because I remember, and I remember that three years later, one dry September evening in 1996, the Taliban captured Kabul; it was our neighbour's son's wedding and the Volga sedan Kaka Aziz, the groom's father, had borrowed to bring the bride home was confiscated. By then grandfather—who lived through the coup of 1929—had been dead five years. Disease, hunger, war, rebellion, riot, earthquake, evacuation, invasion, Taliban, massacre ... goes on the list of events we as a nation hang our memories from. Amid all this, we still like to believe that Alexander the Great said: "God must have loved Afghans because he made them so beautiful."

I don't believe in that claim for an instant. I find it hard to trust a man's dictum of beauty while he gave himself to a life of greed, of razing cities, selling men and women into slavery, and killing anyone who desired to live free. We are beautiful and God hates our guts. That I trust. For us history is not linear, it is the shape of guinea-fowl eggs. We walk on history's hard shell knowing we'll end up where we started. I have reason to trust this as well. Our governments collapse with a regularity and at a rate faster than the earth beneath us can generate seismic waves. And we ride on the tail of this raging beast named the Ring of Fire, an active earthquake belt that circles the Pacific Ocean, starting in Chile, running along the Andes to Aleutians to Japan and Philippine Islands, branching off into the Himalayas and passing through the Hindu Kush.

Our mountains are young and eager and lust for growth, and our wounds are old and forget to heal. Yet we don't speak about the shuddering we feel under our feet, and never about our suffering. We know pain is a language not many people know. We keep things to ourselves and believe in God, but God doesn't believe in us. We wake up in the middle of the night to pray; we fast, sacrifice animals, name our children after deities, light candles in shrines, and make *halva* on Friday evenings and offer it to the hungry. None elicit His pity. Better go in person, we decide, and travel for days to get to Mecca, but God is never home. So we turn to prophets, imams, saints, and sanguinary conquerors for help. Anything they can do to soften His heart of stone. Then come the long spells of drought, clouds of locusts, devastating quakes, and men with unsheathed swords and cocked guns who always happen to have some special message from Him.

The next thing we wish to be sent is an asteroid.

A man who lives near Kabul International Airport says that a dead body fell from the sky over their neighbourhood. There's no terror in his eyes that could possibly be traced back to this event. He goes about it as though airborne corpses are banal occurrences. He's nervous, however, and that's because it's his first time being in front of the camera. His eyes don't know where to look. He stands erect; his voice shakes as he speaks. It seems he is more concerned about his dry mouth than the words his tongue forms to recall the grotesque scene. Somehow he finishes the interview and manages to have a message to the nation: this land is our mother. She needs us. Stay. Don't flee.

Three things occur to me as the news ends and the man's words continue to echo in my head. One, I should go pour myself a glass of something and drink knowingly, as though it were an act of mutiny against thirst. Two, I wish the disgraced President had heard this man prior to boarding that plane to a safe place of clean beaches, good food, and hotel rooms with mattresses that allow 10 percent more *deep sleep*. The third thought is morbid. It concerns the young men who clung on to the sides of a taxiing cargo plane on the first day the government fell and so began the largest civilian evacuation in history. What were the last thoughts that passed through their minds? I ask myself. My imagination has never been good at handling height, or speed. It lags and drifts and is prone to seeking poetry in things. There's poetry in death. But life isn't fair, and not everyone gets to die a poetic death. So I imagine the young men's life before the concept of flight enchanted them. I take their possible memories in my hands like a hunk of potter's clay and mold them to fit my rumination: the excitement of flying a kite, the thrill of learning to ride a bike, the frenzy and elation of youthful love, a dislike for okra, a liking for rain.

These memories are too neat and don't hit hard enough. I want something strong and turn to religion. I wonder if they, the young men, had given the story of Adam and Eve much thought. We studied it in the Quran in the mosque in the winter when schools were off. The tempting fruit? The hand itching with desire? Then Adam and Eve landing on earth? The young men should have remembered that God is an impish child—who teases and testes and likes practical jokes—that that cargo plane was our forbidden fruit, and that our fall from heaven would never be as smooth. For proof, listen to the gruesome details the nervous man gave in his interview with Tolo TV before delivering that message about *flight*.

Afghanistan is a country with four seasons and every season is migration season. Over the years most people that I know have left or dreamed of life elsewhere. One friend is a voice artist. He is the product of the media boom of the early 2000s, when a rare light shone after the dark period of Taliban rule, and radio and television stations sprouted across the country like wildflowers. The network he worked for hired Iranian instructors to train dubbers who could sell foreign soap operas to a local audience that was tired of reality and sought comfort in fictional premises. The other friend is a filmmaker who in 2019 walked onto the red carpet at Cannes Film Festival wearing a white t-shirt that, in black letters on the chest, said: Peace with Taliban = War on Afghan Women.

In the days leading to the fall of Kabul, an Afghan journalist asks the Taliban spokesman in Qatar if they would want to agree to an armistice and give peace talks a chance. There will be no peace without war, the spokesman says. What does that mean? the journalist follows up. And I don't want to know the answer. The peace negotiations continue and so does the war.

Then on Sunday, August 15, 2021, the answer comes to me. Concessions have been made not around the table in Doha, but privately over the phone in Kabul, in the same compound where some presidential palace employees typically go to eat lunch in the dining room. The difference this time is that they enter the dining hall as citizens of the Islamic Republic of Afghanistan and leave as subjects of the new Islamic Emirate.

I check in on my friends. The filmmaker, along with nine members of her family, leave for the airport one night. Their names are on all possible evacuation lists, the French, the Dutch, the American ... What do you see? I ask her in a text. She can't see far. There are too many people, she says. But all night she can hear gunshots. She sends me her location. Then again twelve hours later. They have barely moved, the guns are still hot, the crowd grows minute by minute.

Thousands have gathered in front of the airport. Some have valid passports and visas. Others have brought house-ownership or marriage certificate as possible travel documents. Most have no papers and arrived in the night from the provinces. Then the day breaks and the white sun rises and men, women and children die of heatstroke, of thirst, and in stampedes. One woman, out of sheer frustration and helplessness, looks up to the heavens in front of the camera and wishes death upon Ashraf Ghani's son. If the president lost a child, only then might he feel the pain he has caused the people. But she doesn't understand that even death doesn't dare to enter the president's children's multimillion dollar properties in NYC and Washington, DC. What she does understand is the jaguar sun, lack of water, the rumours of a looming suicide attack, and the armed Taliban fighters who are disappointed that the war is over, and have trained their guns on the sleepless masses who are desperate to flee the country to faraway places where there is hope, life is steady, the grey squirrels resume their frenetic search for food every morning, and there is black coffee and the trees vibrate with the song of cicadas that come out after two decades, their bodies crackling with electricity and the urge to fornicate.

The voice actor and his wife have been going to the airport for four days, but they can't get close enough to a gate to show their documents. The day Kabul fell, I sent him a voice message asking how he was holding up because they, for weeks, had hailed the Afghan forces and made their disgust for the Taliban known via Facebook. Their names were on no evacuation list yet, and the earth was sliding from beneath their feet. His wife was crying nonstop, and he went through three packs of cigarettes in a few desperate, slow-moving hours. His vocal cords were in shock. He could barely talk.

Now their names are safe on the French evacuation roster, and he sends me a picture from somewhere outside the airport. It is Kabul at night, but doesn't seem anything like Kabul nights. There's a strong light entering the right top corner, sending the rest of the frame into darkness populated with human forms whose faces you can't see. "The Day of Reckoning probably looks like this," he texts, alluding to how large and chaotic the crowd is. He adds *hahaha* at the end of his sentence. Hope is a dangerous thing, I say to myself.

My filmmaker friend hasn't seen the message I sent her on WhatsApp. The *Hollywood Reporter*, however, reports that she has told them in an interview that if she survives this, she will make a film about what happened.

Only two weeks earlier, in early August, she and I had talked on the phone for about an hour while I was making vegetable rice noodles in my kitchen in Toronto's west end. She was in her newly bought condo west of Kabul. We discuss the screenplay she is writing, then we joke about some of the popular terminologies that entered Afghanistan with the American dollar in 2001: "proposal writing," "capacity building," "practicing democracy." All of that feels very distant and means nothing now. Those built capacities will soon be stranded behind the airport gates, the practice of democracy will come to a grinding halt, and the proposals were terribly written anyway. While we talk, wildfires rage across the world and the heat in the kitchen is unbearable. I de-seed and mince three red chilies and add them to the pot. I sprinkle the broth with sumac, black pepper and salt, and as it simmers on low heat, I tell her that at the rate the governors are handing over provincial centres, it won't be long before the Taliban capture the capital. I don't quite believe in my own statement. I'm an optimist. But I tell her maybe she should consider coming to Toronto while there are still commercial flights out of Kabul.

She says she will stay until next spring to see how things progress.

The progress is unexpectedly fast. Provinces fall like autumn leaves. National Army soldiers and police die in numbers. The elite Afghan Commandos, often with empty stomachs and no aerial support, are ferried from one corner of the country to the next to stop the advances of the Taliban. Civilians get caught in the crossfire. Some die; those that survive join the ranks of their internally displaced brothers and sisters. Afghans with a roof over their heads—home and abroad—who are convinced of Pakistan's meddling, take the war to the virtual battlefield. #SanctionPakistan flies like bullets.

A high school classmate of mine, a former Afghan diplomat, posts on Facebook that Mr Ghani, along with his national security advisor—a young man with a PhD in 3D design—

and the president's former chief of staff, a man who collected childcare benefits from the Swedish government while being an advisor to the president, are allegedly planning to flee the country with suitcases stuffed with cash.

He creates #ArrestGhani. The hashtag doesn't get traction because the general consensus among Afghans is that the president and his inner circle are morally corrupt, but they are not cowards. Only weeks earlier the president had mocked King Amanullah Khan's flight to Europe a century ago, and in that raspy, shrieking voice of his had said he would stay till the end, "*Da mei kor deh, da mei gor deh*, this country is my home and my grave."

Then Ghani flees. Taliban fighters enter the Presidential Palace and take down the Afghan national flag and put it away. It's televised and feels as if we are getting naked in front of the world, and we are ashamed of what the world sees.

The embarrassment deepens when Mr Ghani puts out a statement on Facebook defending his cowardice. He says that he left so that Kabul doesn't turn into a bloodbath. (By that logic he should have left a long time ago, for Kabul has been a bloodbath since he took office in 2014.) Two days later, in a video, he shifts the blame onto his security team—President Protective Service (PPS). A president who never took advice from anyone, and became known as the Little Dictator among Afghan intelligentsia, now claims he was advised by PPS to leave because there were armed men who spoke none of the country's national languages and were going from room to room in the palace looking for the president. He denies the allegations that he stole cash. He says he didn't even have time to change his sandals for his shoes. Shortly after the video is released, a deputy from the ministry of foreign affairs accuses Mr Ghani of lying. He says that the president knew about his flight days in advance, and had asked the ministry for his passport. Then comes out a list naming fifty-three of the president's aids and staff who boarded that flight alongside him. In an administration as bogged down by corruption and poor communication as his, such an exodus would take days to coordinate.

But the dictator is out, the curtain has come down, and the officials can spill the secrets. In an interview with BBC Persian, Mr Ghani's last chief of staff says that the president was suffering from chronic paranoia, that he viewed his top generals and spy chiefs with suspicion, fearing they would bring him down in a military coup. The war leadership changed so frequently that soldiers on the battlefield could no longer keep track of the chain of command. A woman who served as deputy to the defence minister concurs and tells Afghanistan International television that Mr Ghani only trusted the two young guys close to him. One of them—the man who collected child benefits from the government of Sweden—was put in charge of everything civilian. The other—the one with the PhD in 3D design—controlled everything military and was dreaming of running for president once his boss's term was over. So he installed people in key security posts across the country, and influenced the president's appointments for the cabinet seats. Merit and experience weren't a requirement, the deputy suggests, loyalty and ethnic allegiance were. She and her boss were mere symbols with almost no authority.

They were the lucky ones to have been given a government position, however symbolic. Some political opponents found themselves swatting flies at home, or appearing on talk shows no one watched. Others were introduced to the high court for charges of mutiny, fraud, and, in one particular case, sodomy. Mr Ghani and his inner circle pooled their skills and worked hard to make all that happen. When he first took office, his spokesman—besides boasting that Mr Ghani co-authored a book in which he had fixed failed states—took pride in saying that the president worked sixteen hours each day and took no breaks. Less than two weeks after the American troops pulled out, those long days finally caught up with the president, and not even the theories in his book could save him. He needed somewhere to rest, a place with palm trees, plush pillows, and those mattresses that guarantee deep sleep.

My filmmaker friend arrives in Paris, but she can't sleep. She texts me and says she has left her heart behind in Kabul.

My voice actor friend disagrees. He believes there's nothing left in Kabul, or in the country for that matter, where he remains. The French couldn't evacuate him. His hope withers, and in its empty place, fresh frustration blooms. He goes back to smoking and posting on Facebook. He demands that God send down an asteroid big enough to wipe out the motherland that is Afghanistan. That's one hell of a wish, I say to myself.

As "the world drift away into its madness," I seek refuge in reading Charles Bowden and rising early. There is this belief among the old generation that if you are up and outside when day breaks you will live long. Length of life, like knowing the exact day I was born, doesn't interest me—I know I should have been dead that warm evening during the civil war in 1993 when soldiers shot at us from top of the hill while we played football in the opening down below among the houses—yet I believe in this claim. I know people who have been early risers their entire life and are now so old that they have lost their way to death. I would like to avoid such a fate if I can. I rise early, however, because the plants I keep rely as much on being touched as they do on light and water. I hear the yearning of the dragon tree, the devil's ivy, and the rubber plant. Their lust wakes me. I caress them gently in the dark before I make coffee in the kitchen and go sit out on the balcony to look at the trees; trees that stand still in the backyard with their memories of the past and understanding of the future; trees that I trust have read Borges; they don't speak, not even a rustle, because they know they can't improve the silence.

I like that, and I like this hour of day. The squirrels are asleep. The cicadas are quiet. I sit with black coffee in hand

and think of Afghanistan, of its hardworking, handsome men, its intelligent, ambitious women, its welcoming teashops and food stands, its poetry reading circles, its sunny days and clear nights, and its proud young mountains alive with the roars of untamed snow leopards. It comforts me to know that, before Alexander the Great, the Mongols, and all the invaders who have since arrived and departed, these mountains, lush valleys, cool streams, and vast plains have been here, and will be here until the yellow dwarf dims. It also comforts me to think that time never forgets its habits; that, cut it enough slack, and God will mature and leave us alone; that, blink, and the Taliban will be gone again. I trust that. And I trust that the earth will tremble and tremble, as my mother likes to say, and it will come to rest. Until then I know I have to hold on to that key of patience.

TOIL AND TROUBLE

Stephen Marche

Work isn't working anymore. Covid-19 has thrown off the machinery of twenty-first-century capitalism, and as it stalls and sputters, turning over on its side, the gears and wheels lie open and exposed. This virus has revealed just how far economic theory has diverged from the actual process of earning a living. The unemployment rate is the highest it's been since the Great Depression, while the stock market has rallied well past pre-pandemic levels. The fortunes of America's very richest have risen $406 billion (US) since the outbreak, and as they spend their money on spaceship photo ops, the spectre of hunger stalks the ground they are so desperate to leave behind: 26 million American adults went without meals or relied on charity for groceries last fall, and at least 4.5 million Canadians have experienced food insecurity over the past year. Covid is a disease of the working poor. The failures of the political response, both nationally and internationally, have been failures to address the reality of their working lives.

The value of labour has never been in a more contradictory state. Working men and women—meat packers, farm workers, cashiers, care workers—have proven themselves to be essential as never before. They are the people the system runs on. They are also, apparently, disposable. Covid represents the end of a long road. Middle-class men and women as young as thirty have lived through multiple layoffs already. They know in their bones that their position in society is unrelated to their abilities or their efforts. The notion of lifting oneself up by the bootstraps is for rich kids and people living in the past. The political rhetoric of hard work is like the rhetoric of the family farm. It will not survive much contact with reality.

The question that follows is obvious: What's next? Nobody knows what the future of work looks like in the immediate aftermath of the pandemic—maybe it will go right back to the way it was, or maybe the whole of office culture will evaporate like a tidal pool. But the course of the virus has already shown one obvious fact about how we organize our lives: the countries that were able to stop working, that were able to imagine a value other than the marketplace, had lower death rates than the countries that tried to stay open.

The larger implications of this moment are truly revolutionary. But are we ready for a full re-evaluation of work's place in society? Underlying that political question is a crisis that can be described only as spiritual. Everyone feels it, and for everyone it is personal. Can we learn to value ourselves without working like maniacs?

Donald Trump was the president of 20,000 lies. Barack Obama told two. But Obama's lies mattered more because he is not a liar. Obama's first lie was that America is more united than divided. It isn't. The second was that "if you work hard and play by the rules, you will get ahead." This campaign bromide, repeated dozens of times, was a classic piece of progressive nostalgia—Obama's signature brand. He triangulated conservative and liberal impulses into a fantasy of opportunity. Both impulses were dreams of a world that had passed. Obama's place in history is as the late-coming physician to the

American economy. He worked furiously to cure a patient that was already dead.

The sickness had been long. John Maynard Keynes wrote "Economic Possibilities for Our Grandchildren" in 1930, a moment similar to our own in several key respects. The Depression had arrived, but the memory of unprecedented growth was still alive. The glories of prosperity were fresh in the mind; the shadows of a dark future were looming. In that moment of peril, Keynes found hope against hope. "The disastrous mistakes we have made," he wrote, "blind us to what is going on under the surface—to the true interpretation of the trend of things." His prediction was beyond optimistic: in the long run, "mankind is solving its economic problem."

Yet Keynes also knew that accepting the gift of prosperity would be harder than generating it. A world without work was utopian, not because of the material difficulties but because of the transcendent ones. "There is no country and no people, I think, who can look forward to the age of leisure and of abundance without a dread," he wrote. "For we have been trained too long to strive and not to enjoy."

Our ancestors would find our modern work lives frantically overburdened. During periods of high prosperity, like the fourteenth century, peasants worked as little as 120 days a year. With mid-morning and mid-afternoon breaks, their workdays were rarely longer than eight hours. "For 95 percent of our species' history," the South African anthropologist James Suzman has recently written, "work did not occupy anything like the hallowed place in people's lives that it does now."

The cult of hard work that we know today arose with factories, but it traces its roots back even further. Published in 1905, Max Weber's *The Protestant Ethic and the Spirit of Capitalism* described asceticism, not reason, as the foundation of capitalism. He described a society "dominated by the continually repeated, often almost passionate preaching of hard, continuous bodily or mental labour." For Weber, there were two motives behind the celebration of work rather than its fruits: "Labour is, on the one hand, an approved ascetic technique," connected to monasticism and the defence against sexual temptation. "But the most important thing was that even beyond that labour came to be considered in itself the end of life." With work as an end in itself, capitalism took on a religious dimension: "Unwillingness to work is symptomatic of the lack of grace."

In our own time, the cult of hard work has increased as its validity has declined. There is a whole industry of books that will tell you how you or your children can get ahead: ten thousand hours of practice, or grit, or the ability to pass the marshmallow test, or some other conveniently within-reach mode of self-determination. None of them mention luck or rich parents.

In hindsight, the most risible example of this cult appeared in 2013, in the form of *Lean In: Women, Work, and the Will to Lead*, in which a tech executive argued that women needed to work harder and that their hard work would be rewarded by equality in the end. The myth of pluck and resolve—a world of girl bosses with side hustles—served as a replacement fantasy for necessary public policy. Family leave and mandated board parity are the solutions to women's inequality, but the US government, in particular, is too dysfunctional to enact anything so practical. So instead, the answer, as usual, is that everybody must work harder.

And what was Sheryl Sandberg working so hard for? All her talent, all her brilliance, all her dedication went to serve a company whose primary effect on society is to increase loneliness and depression, and whose political effects have contributed to the decline of democracy. Only a pathological society could promote such a life as a model.

By now, the pathology of pre-pandemic work culture is obvious. In 2016, Lyft actively promoted a story of one of its drivers picking up a fare on the way to give birth to her child. An ad campaign for Fiverr—a marketplace, remember, intended to advertise freelance labour in the way those workers want to be perceived—promoted the risk of mental illness through work: "Sleep deprivation is your drug of choice." The modern exploitation of labour has devolved into outright theft. A 2017 study from the Economic Policy Institute found that, in ten states alone, 2.4 million workers had $8 billion (US) taken from their wages each year. Wage theft within those states alone is roughly half of all property crime in America. Meanwhile, tax evasion, according to research into the Swiss Leaks and the Panama Papers, amounts to nearly 30 percent of the taxes owed by the top 0.01 percent.

Nonetheless the cult of hard work persists. Conspicuous consumption has been replaced by conspicuous labour. The perception of busyness is an elite human capital characteristic. It's all a joke, and a thinning joke at that. The younger you are, the less funny it is. The difference among the outcomes of individuals' lives is not mainly in how much one works. It's mainly in how much one is given. Conspicuous labour is an all too transparent cover for the newly dominant rentier reality.

Everyone will have to come to an individual reckoning with the new futility. Already in Japan, during a long period of economic stagnation, there emerged a group of individuals, dubbed the "herbivore men," who became famous as sexless introverts. Western media accounts, almost all brief and focused on the sex, missed the point of the herbivore lifestyle. Their refusal was more general and more widespread. They refused the life of the salaryman. They refused to participate in a system of achievement in which karoshi, or "death by overwork," is a serious enough problem that the government long ago established a hotline to combat it. The herbivore men decided to vote with their lives and with their sperm. Japan now has the lowest number of births since record keeping began.

Again, Covid-19 has been a revelation: after the onset of the disease, suicide rates in Japan declined by 20 percent, but then they surged past pre-Covid levels. The system doesn't need indictment. It indicts itself. The culture of hard work is an exploitative practice of self-destruction. John Henry died with a hammer in his hand.

The pandemic has revealed the pathology of our work lives. It also offers a tantalizing opportunity to reformulate the value of labour, both in ourselves and in the public sphere. "The economic problem is not—if we look into the future—the permanent problem of the human race," Keynes wrote nine decades ago. "It will be those peoples, who can keep alive, and cultivate into a fuller perfection, the art of life itself and do not sell themselves for the means of life, who will be able to enjoy the abundance when it comes."

The moment has come to ask what the point is—why we're doing all this work. Policies are emerging that value humanity over the labour it can produce. These policies have not been formulated into a party or even a platform but are growing in strength, outside the boundaries of the traditional left or right. The solution to the future of industrial capitalism can be summarized in a phrase: the world needs a politics of laziness.

Countries across Europe have already begun implementing greatly reduced workweeks with stunning effects. France, in 2000, reduced weekly hours to thirty-five. In Holland, the average workweek is now twenty-nine hours. Sweden has begun to experiment with six-hour workdays. Companies report greater productivity. Workers report vastly improved well-being.

But paying the same for less labour is only a beginning. The real hope of the politics of laziness is the separation of work from its fruits altogether: money for nothing. Universal basic income is no longer a purely utopian concept. In many countries, it would be little more than an extension of what has already been put in place during Covid—easily accessible payment for people who stayed home. Canada has historically been a leader in universal basic income, going back to a social experiment in Manitoba in the 1970s. And now the idea is starting to take hold in hyper-capitalist places like Los Angeles. Recently the mayor, Eric Garcetti, outlined a proposal to give thousands of dollars in direct monthly payments to homeless people in his city. The program would be relatively small—$24 million (US)—but it shows an unprecedented willingness to hand over cash to people who have done nothing to earn it.

These are teases, though—hints, suggestions, small-scale tests. Only radical policies have any hope of slowing down spiralling inequality. Those policies will require massive change. With *Capital and Ideology*, the French economist Thomas Piketty joins a long line of thinkers—stretching back through Keynes to Karl Marx himself—who have convinced themselves that the vast prosperity of exploitative capitalism can be redirected to the liberation of human potential. His plans include transnational government bodies to oversee taxation and "a capital endowment to be given to each young adult (at age 25, say), financed by a progressive tax on private wealth." Literally, you'd get an inheritance for being a person. This policy is feasible on a fiscal level; the question is whether wealthy countries can find the will.

Embracing laziness goes against all of our most ingrained instincts, which is why it will be so difficult, perhaps impossible to actually achieve. The question of labour and its value transcends the grandest questions of political and economic organization. It amounts to a spiritual revaluation of value itself. Can we escape the myths we have built around money and self-worth?

The myths of labour will be hard to escape because they lie deep in ourselves. The cult of hard work offers individuals a profound and grounding myth of self-generation: the belief that, through inner forces, they may triumph over the world. This myth is so powerful, so innate, that anyone steeped in it cannot abandon it: Nobody gave me anything. I made my own life. It's a beautiful thing to be able to think about your-self, but, if it was ever true, it was true only in the past.

The world, as it is coming to be, will require new ways to value ourselves, ways that are different from earning a living. In "Economic Possibilities for Our Grandchildren," Keynes quoted a traditional charwoman's epitaph, which imagined paradise as permanent inactivity: "Don't mourn for me, friends, don't weep for me never / For I'm going to do nothing for ever and ever."

But there was a second part to the cleaning lady's epitaph, which is perhaps sadder: "With psalms and sweet music the heavens'll be ringing, / But I shall have nothing to do with the singing."

The cult of hard work has destroyed, for the charwoman, any impulse to contribute. That would be the most terrible sacrifice to the ancient cult of labour for labour's sake. We will need ways of shaping the earth other than vacillating between frenzy and emptiness. The world may not owe you a living, but you don't owe the world your being either.

KLEIN BOTTLE

Heather Jessup

The book on how to write a novel tells me that for the next three months I should not engage in any other projects: don't get married, divorced, build an addition to your house, or move across the country. What about a baby? I wonder. What about writing a novel while pumping breast milk, folding tiny socks, bouncing a carrier, and having Cheerios stuck in your hair? What about coaxing the soft heap of your postpartum body up and into the shower? What about teaching a child how to be?

In topology, a branch of mathematics, both the Möbius strip and the Klein bottle are examples of non-orientable surfaces. A Klein bottle can be created by affixing together two Möbius strips that are mirror images of each other into a single-sided bottle with no boundary. Orientability is a property of all geometric surfaces in Euclidean space. Euclidean space is the space of classical geometry: the ideas of dimensionality and orientation that are taught in high school while students scrunch themselves over workbooks to find the y axis of a two-dimensional triangle or a three-dimensional prism. But a Klein bottle is a non-orientable manifold. A Klein bottle is an example of a one-sided surface that, if travelled upon, can be

followed back to the point of origin while flipping the travel-
ler upside down.

We saw the pediatric nurse at a wedding reception, and
I am not even sure that I would have remembered her face,
except that I recognized the mole. It is a rather large mole. Not
unattractive. A beauty mark. She is the woman who gently slid
the blood-soaked hospital underwear down each of my legs.
Before my child was born, she monitored his heart. She is the
one who tells me to take the morphine and draws a tally on
a whiteboard by the hospital bed of how many days we have
been in the room. It is a room with a window, so we are lucky.
Outside the window we can see the blazing fall leaves, the blue
sky, and our apartment building up the lane in the West End.
The building is remote, grey, and abstract.

In the apartment there are twenty unripe tomatoes sitting
on top of an old library card catalogue. I picked them green
from our garden three days before the baby was born. My plan
was to put up a green chow relish I learned when I lived on
the East Coast. But these tomatoes are my initiation into time
passing and into disappointment. I will learn to abandon my
own desires and creative enterprises, particularly the kind
that take hours, boiling-hot liquid, and breakable glass jars.
These tomatoes will begin to rot while we are in the hospital.
When we arrive home, I will bend slowly down to pick up the
compost pail, careful not to rip my stitches, and gently place
each decaying tomato in the bucket, one by one.

The book on how to write a novel has no advice regarding
how to become a non-orientable manifold. The book includes
a diagram of a three-act structure, and there are helpful sections on how the protagonist will experience false hope and
will then suffer, surrender, and return home, but there is no
mention of how you must stir one part apricot juice into
one part lemon verbena tea, blend with two tablespoons of
almond butter and castor oil, and then wait until your weakness appears to you as a strength so overlooked it is the riddle

of a Klein bottle. The book does not tell you that you must pry yourself out of your ordinary life—of sleeping, of brunch, of bathing, of remembering birthdays or the names of your own cousins, of returning the email or finishing the thank-you cards, of finding the stamps and addressing an envelope—lowering yourself out of this hot air balloon that you've been travelling along in, unaware, this whole time. How you must step out of the basket, mid-air, and descend on a rope ladder over a desert and some mountain ranges, a river with a name written in elfin serifs, and then hang there over the decorative calligraphic legend of the map itself. This is the method of travel best suited to meeting a baby. These are the territories you must visit to write your next book. But you must be sure you are still able to find the rope ladder at the end of the lake woods through the dark peaty forest so you can remind yourself to get to the daycare on time or to start dinner or to climb back into yourself so no one notices you were gone.

Klein bottles can be physically realized only in four dimensions. The novel I want to write begins in Spain and takes place in three dimensions. The story is as old as Euclidean geometry: young woman is an Andalucían flamenco-dancing underwater mermaid performer; young woman finds true love; young woman must sacrifice her subaquatic life to raise her child in a landlocked town far from her home. The book on how to write a novel is not currently helping me. I turn over my magic eight ball, and Zadie Smith answers instead, like her voice is on speakerphone inside my head. "Writers do not write what they want to write. They write what they can." "Resign yourself to the lifelong sadness that comes from never being satisfied." Every attempt to fashion a Klein bottle on earth will inevitably fail because we are bound by the restriction of existing in three dimensions. To meet a baby, you must become a non-orientable surface where weakness is the strongest bonding agent connecting an orbit of physical beings in one room. You must have no boundary. You must welcome the fragility of this new baby and of your own mortal body to become who you are about to become. To write a book, you must undergo a process whereby you coax inside into being outside, knowing this dimensionality will always be an approximation.

I hold the baby against my chest and stare out the window. For three days I have been looking at our apartment building up the hill. I do not yet have the doctor's permission to go home so I picture inside our apartment on the sixth floor. There are brightly coloured cushions on the couch. On the edge of the claw-foot bathtub is a new bar of lavender shea soap. There is a large mason jar of homemade butternut-squash soup waiting in the fridge. In the kitchen cupboard above the stove is the coffee percolator I have carried with me from city to city ever since living in Montreal. That coffee maker and I once made a book. Now my husband and I have made a baby. From the hospital room, the apartment feels like a non-orientable surface. When my husband goes to get the laptop from the apartment so we can make the birth announcement, it feels as though he has travelled to another country, where I once lived but where I have not been in a long time. He has entered another dimension. He is gone for twenty minutes.

The day we are released from the hospital, we walk home. We push the baby up the lane in the bassinet stroller. We pass a miniature Spider-Man holding onto an adult's hand. Twin child-pirates wave, hanging off of a play structure in the back-yard of the neighbourhood daycare. A mouse with painted-on whiskers and a lightning-tailed Pikachu yell to the others: "It's a baby! It's a tiny new baby!" They have confirmed you as an initiate into their world. Today is the human custom of Halloween. We are about to welcome you home. My husband turns the key in the lock, and the threshold is a looking-glass world where everything we ever owned is made unfamiliar. I walk around making introductions between myself, the baby, and reality. "This is our apartment. This is where you live now. Here's where we take off our shoes. Here are the books. Here is the window. A window is a place where light comes in and you can see out to the city where you were born. Here's the record player. Here is Bach's *Goldberg Variations*. This man who plays the piano is called Glenn Gould. Here's blue. Here is night-time. Here's a bath. Here is your dada's voice as he reads to you in the rocking chair."

The nurse's name is Oleander. When we see her at the wedding reception, my child is eight months old and has just peed through the adorable tiny suit with a bowtie he was wearing for the occasion. We changed him on the backseat of the rental car in the blazing summer sun, and so now he is wearing the ugly spare change of clothes from his diaper bag—a striped pair of pants and a tiny, wrinkled T-shirt—and for some reason I find myself explaining all of this to Oleander, wanting her to know why our child isn't properly dressed for a wedding. Oleander tells us that she is not nursing this year, and I understand this to mean she is not breastfeeding. "I've taken a year-long leave. I'm flying to Greece to certify as a yoga instructor." My sleep deprivation is so acute that none of the words Oleander has spoken to me make sense. First of all, I had completely forgotten about the existence of the country Greece. Recalling it now—Parthenon, sky-blue water, white-washed windmills, Euclidean geometry—it is as if a Hellenic Republic has sprung from Oleander's forehead like a dream. Second, I am picturing a yoga instructor holding up a police badge, but then remember that the signified *police badge* is not what is meant by the signifier *certification*, and although I realize that the words and the pictures of the book in my head do not match, I want desperately to know how our nurse has found the time for pilot lessons.

The book on how to write a novel tells me I should avoid renovating a kitchen. I should not attempt travel. Please ensure that all friends, family members, and colleagues avoid being diagnosed with cancer. I should not have a job, nor should I compile a sixty-page teaching dossier to apply for a different job in a faraway city where I could possibly write. My parents should not age. I should not have to transition my child to daycare. I should not have to wean. The book tells me that as I enter into the midst of the novel, I may experience a shift in my priorities. Sometimes, the book warns, my friends and family will not take kindly to these changes. This does not mean I am bad or selfish. It just means the garbage will get taken out tomorrow. Which is all fine—and impossible.

What I really want the book to tell me is how to unfasten my Möbius strip from my child's Möbius strip so that we can be released from our configuration as each other's Klein bottle, reassuming once again a three-dimensional manifold, or, dare I dream, whereby we can once again embody a Euclidean concept of space in which our orientable surfaces can consistently be defined. The book does not say that this release will be ecstatic and anguishing, that my child will walk into his first day at daycare wearing his planetary bike helmet and his rainbow-strapped blue backpack with swaggering self-assurance on Monday and screaming separation anxiety on Tuesday, and that both of these diagrams of distance will make me muffle-cry into a bouquet of cheap toilet paper in a stall in the college's staff bathroom because, never mind, I don't want to teach again or write anything ever at all; I just want to spend every brief moment I have watching the movements of his small determined body. No, forget that, all I need is to be alone and to not be constantly touched and required, and—Come on now, which is it? Choose.

The book forgets to mention that this unfastening of our Klein bottle into two distinct Möbius strips will be as if wailed from the throat of the cantaora while the flamenco dancer's fingers drag the pain of the stars out of the sky with her Siguiriya, beginning on the day of the child's birth and then taking approximately three years, give or take the rest of the writer's life.

The book on how to write a novel fails to inform us that we will become actors in an apocalyptic movie filmed at the airport when I decide I must move my entire family across the country to take the job where I can possibly write. In this movie, there are a hundred students trying to return to their hometowns in China. The airline staff assessing their documents in the ticket lineup are dressed in hazmat suits. Except for this line of students, and our possessions piled into an approximation of a blanket fort on our dolly, the airport is empty. The clock tells time, but it is unclear what time is. All of our wristwatches break. Numbers become extinct. We are leaving the ski hill lights on the mountains and the cherry blossoms. We are leaving daffodils and two godchildren that bloom by the bay in January.

Our destination, this city we now live in, is covered in snow cast from the spell of a witch who is wearing a mask and sweeping her front steps with a broom. We came by airplane, or steam-powered paddle boat, or holding onto the long neck of an excavator or a dinosaur. We were carried by the song of the loneliest whale, whose pitch other whales can't hear, so it calls and calls and is never answered. My husband is the one who tells me about this whale. "How do they know it's lonely? What if it just likes to sing on its own?" I ask. "I don't know," he tells me. "There's a body of literature about this on the internet." He says, "I can share a podcast with you." My whole family has moved across the country so I can wonder about the loneliness of a whale.

Just like that our baby is three years old and can talk in full sentences and pose difficult questions. This morning he asks: "How do I get inside of the book?" He opens a book about space, or what machines do, or the one about a turtle not knowing what to get his mother for her birthday. He places the book onto the living-room rug, pages opened wide, and takes one step and then another onto the picture. I imagine him falling in, disappearing, and me picking up the book to find my child orbiting in space with the blue light of Neptune shining on his face, or spinning around in a washing machine, or at the mother turtle's bedside, bringing her breakfast and a homemade brooch made from a button. This is what I want to know too. How do I get inside the book I am writing? But my child is still there, standing in our living room on top of a library book, and I say, "We don't stand on books. We want to keep the pages smooth for the other children." I tell him, "Don't put the string around your throat." "Don't eat the white berries. They are only for the birds." "Don't stand on the wobbly side table to put your magnifying glass on the tallest shelf." He asks, "Why?" I answer, "Because the ultimate Möbius strip attached to all of our Möbius strips that allows us to become Klein bottles and enter into another dimension is death." Then the novel wanting to be written asks me "Why?" "Because I made you, and fed you, and kept you alive for all this time, and I want you to live."

I tell my child that if we want to know how to get inside the book, we should ask our new neighbour, Naheer, who lives across the street, because he is a mathematical genius who also plays the piano and is working in a virtual-reality lab, or maybe it's an artificial-intelligence lab, or some kind of Euclidean-geometry lab at the university. Maybe he can help. Now my child believes—and so do I, a little bit—that Naheer might be able to play the right key on his piano and we will slip inside of a book and wind ourselves through the gears of an automated ticket booth at the train station or understand the buoyancy of Saturn or draw a birthday card for our mother turtle, or perhaps I will finally know the music of what it feels like for my protagonist to leave her home in Almería, and the ocean, and her mother. Always her homesickness is for her mother, and why do all of the Andalusian flamenco songs long for a mother in all of their pain?

At the wedding reception, Oleander says goodbye by whispering the mathematical equation for a Klein bottle. Soon it will be two o'clock in the afternoon, and we must put the baby to bed.

"$(x2 + y2 + z2 + 2y - 1) [(x2 + y2 + z2 - 2y - 1)2 - 8z2] + 16xz (x2 + y2 + z2 - 2y - 1) = 0$," Oleander assures me. But all I can hear is *zzzz*, which makes me fall asleep at the table and wake up in the car.

Here are twenty tomatoes that we picked from the garden, my belly a scooped-up and well-patted mound of dirt. Here is the book I am reading on how to write a novel. Here is your blanket. Here are the gulls crying. Here is the day moon. Maybe, I begin to wonder, to be writing means to be rewritten. I am only just now starting to learn. Here is a blade of grass. Here is a dandelion. Here is a sailboat unmoored from its anchor and run gently aground. Here is the sound of your dada breathing in his sleep. He picked you up from school today so that I could write this down. His breath is the song the loneliest whale hears from deep in the ocean and sings back to in reply. Here are children. You are a child. Here is the world, in case you were sleeping the first time you came home.

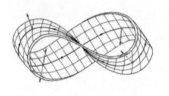 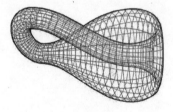

The book on how to write a novel throughout this piece is loosely based on *The 90-Day Novel* by Alan Watt (90-day novel press, 2017), which is a book that, while not always conducive to the life of a parent or caregiver, I have actually found lovely, and useful, and which I would recommend.

The pictured model of the Möbius strip is from: Sheng, Xichen. "1963 Möbius Strip" *Medium*. medium.com/

designscience/1963-88a359d2f68b. Accessed February 5, 2021. The model of the Klein bottle is from the faculty page of Professor Emeritus Steven Edwards. "Math 4596 Topology." *Kennesaw State University*. facultyweb.kennesaw.edu/sedwar77/4596.php. Accessed February 5, 2021. Where Professor Edwards also includes this joke: "Why did the chicken cross the Möbius Strip? To get to the same side."

Part of the description of the Klein Bottle in the second paragraph comes from: "Klein Bottle." *Wikipedia*. Accessed February 5, 2021.

Zadie Smith's advice is affixed together from two of her *Guardian* columns: "This is how it feels to me." theguardian.com/books/2001/oct/13/fiction.afghanistan. and "Rules for Writers." theguardian.com/books/2010/feb/22/zadie-smith-rules-for-writers. Both last accessed February 5, 2021.

BLIND SPOTS

Christopher Cheung

I can't find the city I know in the newspapers. Anyone who doesn't speak English or is too busy working isn't invited to speak on the radio. Their lives are rarely on the evening news because TV crews drive past their neighbourhoods unless there's a crime to be covered. As for the newer outlets that have staked out a place online—the ones that maimed the free weeklies and captured the ad money that kept them alive— they're more concerned with "The 14 Hottest Patios to Hit Up this Summer!" than they are with keeping citizens informed and engaged.

I came to this realization thanks to my grandfather's vegetable garden. All my life I've eaten the chayotes, green beans and winter melons he tends to every morning. He's lived off his garden since before I was born.

My grandfather isn't the only one in the neighbourhood who grows vegetables. Many are Cantonese like us. Mr Chow with his wax gourds. Mrs Chang with her bitter melons. Others are immigrants from different parts of the world who landed here and started growing things on Vancouver soil, like Mr Stubos from Greece, who lives across the street from my grandfather with his giant tomatoes and sour cherries. Over the years, this band of neighbours has chatted over garden fences and shared seeds and harvests with each other.

When I lived in other parts of the city, the story was the same, though with different characters. Mrs Fung with her Szeyap bitter greens. Auntie Mee Mee with her goji berries. The shy Portuguese couple with the beautiful, enviable figs. On evening walks in the summer, I wouldn't see a single street or alley without these lush gardens and some retiree tending to them, often with a grandchild helping.

Imagine my surprise, then, when I opened up the *Sun*, our daily paper, and read about how Vancouver is catching up with other North American cities experiencing an urban farming "renaissance."

Renaissance? These yards have been feeding Vancouverites since before I was born. Curious about what this renaissance might entail, I read on.

The story, one of many on this subject, celebrated gardens that were the result of city-sanctioned efforts, with tech firms and young urbanites looking to consummate a green lifestyle. It was farming by the Brooklyn playbook that has gone viral from city to city—not a made-in-Vancouver approach. One such urban farmer interviewed by *Montecristo* magazine said that most homeowners' lawns are about decoration for "leisure value or visual appeal." He boasted about his "resistance," "challenging" the idea of what a yard could be if it were farmed. He and others went on to talk about "reconnecting" people with food systems and their neighbours in this grand effort.

Obviously, these new Vancouver farmers hadn't checked their own city to see if what they were doing was new. Google Street View could have told them. If this was, as they called it, a "resistance," then my grandfather and thousands of urban farmers like him were original overthrowers of the status quo, one melon at a time.

I once thought journalism was a reliable reflection of reality. Nowadays, I can't help but view reporting as a reflection of whoever happens to be holding the pen, and they aren't representing or writing about large parts of the community. Journalists may aspire to gather and report the truth, but what good is that if they don't interrogate their own blind spots?

I am troubled by the stories that are told in Vancouver, where I live. In many of our neighbourhoods, "visible minorities" are actually the majority. In my former area of Victoria-Fraserview, we "minorities" represented 84 percent of the population. Yet the diversity that has defined our port city since colonization isn't reflected in the media. I see many local journalists either ignore cultural diversity or exoticize people and places with an outsider's gaze, a gaze that often dehumanizes poorer folks as well.

Data on the diversity of Canadian journalists is lacking, though one study by a Ryerson professor in 2006 found that only 3.4 percent of working journalists were Indigenous or people of colour. If it's the usual suspects doing the news-gathering, it's no surprise they return with the usual stories.

Media is supposed to be a pillar of democracy. But what good is reporting if it paints an incomplete picture of our society, always showing the same groups of people with the same perspectives in its pages?

I can understand how certain populations are left out of the news. Maybe they don't speak English. Maybe they're busy working or caring for their families. Maybe they're unfamiliar with local media. Maybe they live in areas that journalists know nothing about. Hey, maybe they were in the shower when a reporter called.

But that's exactly why journalists need to work harder to pursue stories that are truly representative—to speak other languages, to work around other people's commitments, to fully inform sources about how interviews will be used, to get to know places the way locals do. How else would people feel that they have a share in local institutions? How else would they feel that society is better when they speak up?

I remember one of the first questions we discussed in journalism school. It was an existential one: what is news? One definition was that news is information that is new. But I had a followup: new to whom?

The *National Post* once carried a story about congee that began like this: "Want a delicious new way to eat rice? As in, a way that doesn't involve eating it from a little white takeout box?" The writer seemed unaware that congee is three thousand years old, or that rice exists outside Panda Express. English language media often has this western gaze, scouting out ancient cultures to discover. My friend joked that I should write an article about toast, the delicious new way to eat bread.

The CBC once ran a profile of a cocaine user living in Vancouver's impoverished Downtown Eastside. The writer tried to surprise us with the news that the subject was a grandparent who even had "doilies on the coffee table." It was news for a person so privileged that they couldn't imagine someone who uses drugs as a human being with a family.

The "new to whom?" question took a disturbing turn in the coverage of entrepreneurs opening restaurants and boutiques to create a "new" neighbourhood called Fraserhood. The local alt-weekly *Georgia Straight* floated the idea that it could have been called "Little Portland" for its hipness, quoting a business owner who said the area is finally becoming "more of a community." And *Vancouver Magazine* reported that before adventurous creatives made it a worthwhile destination, it was a "no-man's land."

There was no mention that the area has been a vibrant community since the Second World War, with waves of immigrants from Germany, Austria, Poland, Vietnam, and the Philippines making a home there. Or that the neighbourhood has an existing name, Mountainview. I interviewed a man named Andre Matuszewski who immigrated in 1979, and he recalled visiting the neighbourhood's Polish deli for a comforting sandwich before popping next door for a bowl of pho.

There was a colonial attitude of *terra nullius* to the coverage, assuming that blue-collar immigrant neighbourhoods did not exist and ignoring the significance of these places to Indigenous people before settlers paved them over.

It would be unfair to say that journalism in Vancouver is all like this—devoid of the poor, the working class or people of colour. But when there is coverage, it often plays to a number of tropes.

One boilerplate is the one about the model minority. You know, the quirky immigrant who doesn't speak much English but loves Canada and works hard to serve his community and provide for his family. There is a profile in the *Vancouver Courier* of an elderly Cantonese couple who retired but then "wanted to work," and now serve "cheap food" to locals at an "unpolished" diner. The quotes make them seem overly sacrificial, "doing my good job," the husband says, to "get a life no trouble" and send his children to university. There are many of these heartwarming stories in community papers, showcasing poster patriots who believe in the Canadian dream. But these immigrants seem cartoonish, without complex humanity, and the stories promote a simplistic idea that hard work is all it takes for a newcomer to succeed—no government assistance needed—and those who don't succeed simply need to pull themselves up by their bootstraps.

Another trope is the exotic destination. That's the one where the author points excitedly to a place that's off the beaten path, without regard for those who frequent it. *Daily Hive* once published an article on Jack's Place, a sandwich counter inside a century-old downtown department store. "Now when we say bargain, we mean it . . . they are basically free," the author wrote, adding that it was "grungy." It was written for tourists on the hunt for cheap eats, but the no-frills counter is actually a treasured spot in a neighbourhood for homeless people and low-income renters. Without full kitchens, or a kitchen at all, they come to enjoy a hot meal on a budget. There is a long history of journalism romanticizing places like this for the grit and adventure while ignoring the people they're actually for, or turning them into colourful wallpaper.

There are also tropes portraying the poor and people of colour as victims and villains. I encounter reductionist coverage about ethnic Chinese like me on the regular. Chinese people spat on. Chinese people beaten up. Chinese investors with poor architectural taste. Chinese businesses unwilling to add English to their signs. The stories are shallow, with behaviour implied to be a characteristic of Chinese identity, and often lack interviews with the very Chinese people that are being written about. When global-minded publications like the *Guardian*, *Mother Jones* and the *New Yorker* came to town to write features about Chinese nationals buying Vancouver real estate, not a single one of them interviewed a Chinese buyer.

I became a journalist to counter simplistic narratives like these. I wanted to listen to underrepresented people and showcase what they had to say on their own terms. I wanted to use writing as a way for people in my city to have a voice, and for my neighbours to understand who they share this place with.

I pitched a story that had been on my mind for a long time to the *Vancouver Courier*. You can probably guess what it was about: profiles of immigrant urban farmers like my grandfather, to set the record straight.

They were easy to find and chat with, but hard to convince to talk on the record. I just wanted them to spill the beans on their beans, but the answers I received echoed the same theme.

"This is nothing special. Everyone does this."

"I'm not an expert! You should ask an expert."

"Why do you find this interesting?"

I would hear these answers again and again when I interviewed immigrants and low-income people for other stories. One was about immigrant families living with three generations under one roof. It was such a normal thing for them that they wondered why I thought it was worth a story.

As I chatted with them, it became evident that they had a lot to share, but they didn't think people would care to read about their lives. "You should interview a professor instead," one told me. Others would agree to an interview, but decline to share their name. "Why do you need my name?" they'd say. "I'm a nobody."

I began to worry that underrepresented subjects had internalized the belief that mainstream media in their city was not for or about them.

I recently wrote about Vancouver's only "Filipino Town," which is about to lose half of its businesses to a new condo tower, spurred by a city plan for increased density. Gone will be the corner store where workers, often with multiple jobs, wired earnings to their families in the Philippines. Gone will be the cheap canteens where pandemic frontliners without time to cook picked up food for the week. When I walked through the area with a Filipino-Canadian advocate who raised a family there, he shared an all-too-common attitude locals have about the impending destruction of this village square: "That's just how it is."

A young organizer told me about a similar response she heard from older Vietnamese Vancouverites when she asked them about government policy. "If something happens, I'll just have to accept it," said one elder after another. When Covid-19 hit, seeing the lack of translated messaging for them infuriated her. Was being left behind something to be endured when their livelihoods were concerned? "They shouldn't have to accept that," she told me.

I see a self-fulfilling prophecy at work here. If journalists don't make an effort to seek out underrepresented communities, they won't know that their experiences are worth sharing, or that what they say has the power to shape society.

Our democracy needs this plurality. Difference should not be measured from a baseline of privilege. The stories I most often read about my city are Vancouver as yogadom, bike mecca, cannabis central, Left Coast and Hollywood North. Homeless or racialized people can't be sprinkled into the coverage as supporting characters or exceptions to the norm. This is their city too, and they deserve to be in the spotlight—their trials, their triumphs, their day-to-day routines. Where do they stop for a bite? How do they make ends meet? What are their dreams?

If journalists don't get to know the people they serve, why would they ever want to share anything?

There is a joke in journalism school that the millennials and Gen Zs entering the profession are too afraid to pick up the phone. Pity democracy if they never even leave the office.

CONTRIBUTORS' BIOGRAPHIES

Jamaluddin Aram is a writer from Kabul, Afghanistan. His works have appeared in *Numero Cinq*, *The Write Launch*, *Cagibi*, and the *Globe and Mail*. Aram's short story "This Hard Easy Life" was a finalist for RBC Bronwen Wallace Award for Emerging Writers in 2020. His debut novel, *Nothing Good Ever Happens in Wazirabad on Wednesday*, is forthcoming from Scribner Canada in 2023. Aram has a bachelor's degree in English and history from Union College in Schenectady, New York. He lives in Toronto.

Sharon Butala has published twenty-one books of fiction and nonfiction, earning her three Governor General's nominations, a Commonwealth Writers Prize shortlisting, and a Rogers Writers' Trust Fiction prize shortlisting, among others. She has also had five plays produced, published numerous essays and articles, and given many talks on various subjects from creativity to grasslands life. Among the many awards given her are the Marian Engel Award, the Cheryl and Henry Kloppenburg Award for Literary Excellence, and the W O Mitchell/City of Calgary Award, and with her husband, three conservation awards. She is an Officer in the Order of Canada, is invested in the Saskatchewan Order of Merit, and has three honorary doctorates. At eighty-two, she continues to write and publish, often these days, about the joys and difficulties of being elderly while still trying to have a life. Thus, ageism haunts her, and she writes about it too.

Kunal Chaudhary was a finalist for the Best Emerging Writer title at the 2022 National Magazine Awards. His writing has appeared in publications such as *Spacing Magazine*, the *West End Phoenix*, and the *National Observer*. Currently, he works as an investigative journalist at the Humber College StoryLab, where he is part of an inter-disciplinary team researching hate crimes across Canada. He is based in Toronto.

Christopher Cheung is a journalist who writes about urban change, inequality, housing, diasporas, and food in Vancouver, where he lives. He is currently a staff reporter at *The Tyee*. Cheung has also written for many other publications and won multiple awards. Most recently, he was recognized by BC's Jack Webster Foundation for a series on race and the pandemic. He interviewed immigrant workers overrepresented among frontline jobs, showcased citizen efforts to provide language translation that health authorities didn't, and crunched data to prove that it was racialized, blue-collar neighbourhoods that were hardest hit by Covid-19—information the province did not provide to the public. Cheung holds a Master of Journalism from the University of British Columbia.

Emma Gilchrist is co-founder and editor-in-chief of *The Narwhal*, an award-winning online magazine that publishes in-depth and investigative journalism about Canada's natural world. *The Narwhal* is a pioneer of non-profit journalism in Canada and has grown from a staff of two to a staff of twenty-two in the four years since its launch. Before founding *The Narwhal*, Emma worked at newspapers and magazines in the UK and Canada. Emma's essay, originally published in *Maisonneuve*, won gold at the 2022 National Magazine Award for personal journalism. When Emma is not tethered to her computer, she is happiest surfing the waves of Vancouver Island and Central America.

Michelle Good is a Cree writer and a member of the Red Pheasant Cree Nation in Saskatchewan. After working for Indigenous organizations for twenty-five years, she obtained a law degree and advocated for residential school survivors for over fourteen years. Good earned a Master of Fine Arts in Creative Writing at the University of British Columbia while still practising law and managing her own law firm. Her poems, short stories, and essays have been published in magazines and anthologies across Canada, and her poetry was included on two lists of the best Canadian poetry in 2016 and 2017. *Five Little Indians*, her first novel, won the HarperCollins/UBC Best New Fiction Prize, the Amazon First Novel Award, the Governor General's Literary Award, the Rakuten Kobo Emerging Writer Award, the Evergreen Award, the City of Vancouver Book of the Year Award, and Canada Reads 2022. It was also longlisted for the Scotiabank Giller Prize and a finalist for the Writers' Trust Award, the Ethel Wilson Fiction Prize, and the Jim Deva Prize for Writing that Provokes. Most recently, in October 2022, Simon Fraser University conferred upon her an Honorary Doctor of Letters.

Paul Howe is a professor of political science at the University of New Brunswick in Fredericton, where he has taught since 2001. Prior to joining UNB, he was a research director at the Montreal-based Institute for Research on Public Policy for three years.

The health of modern democracy has been a key focus of his research. Among other topics, he has written about declining voter participation and civic literacy among younger Canadians, electoral reform in New Brunswick, and democratic deconsolidation in the United States. His book *Citizens Adrift: The Democratic Disengagement of Young Canadians* (UBC Press 2010) was awarded the 2011 Donald Smiley Prize by the Canadian Political Science Association for the best English-language book in Canadian politics and government.

His most recent work, *Teen Spirit: How Adolescence Transformed the Adult World* (Cornell University Press 2020), takes a broader look at patterns of social, political, and cultural change in modern society and their connection to the animating ethos of adolescence.

Jane Hu is a writer and PhD graduate from UC-Berkeley.

Heather Jessup is the Creative Writing Program Coordinator at Dalhousie University. She is the author of the novel *The Lightning Field*, and a book on truth, lies, and art called *This Is Not a Hoax: Unsettling Truth in Canadian Culture*. She is the co-curator of the national exhibition *Make Believe: The Secret Library of M. Prud'homme—A Rare Collection of Fakes*. She lives in Halifax, Nova Scotia on the unceded territories of Mi'kma'ki.

Chafic LaRochelle holds a BSc in neuroscience and works as a technical writer in Montreal. He's an avid outdoorsman and volunteer search and rescue (SAR) technician. His prose has previously appeared in *The Fiddlehead*.

Stephen Marche is a writer who lives in Toronto with his wife and children. His most recent book is *The Next Civil War*.

Kathy Page's personal essays have appeared in a variety of journals and anthologies. Her most recent novel, *Dear Evelyn*, winner of the 2018 Rogers Writers' Trust Award for Fiction, concerns a seventy-year marriage between incompatible partners. The UK *Guardian* described it as "a love story, a coming-of-age story, and a brilliantly evocative sketch of Britain in the 20th century." According to the *TLS*, "Page has laid bare the lives of her characters, making no claims as to their significance to anyone but each other, and in doing so has demonstrated that the ordinary is infinitely precious." Her short-story collections *Paradise & Elsewhere* and *The Two of Us* were each nominated for the Scotiabank Giller Prize. She is the author of seven other novels, including *The Story of My Face*, nominated for the (Orange) Women's Prize; *The Find*, a ReLit finalist; and *Alphabet*, a Governor General's Award finalist. Born in the UK, Page moved with her family to Salt Spring Island in British Columbia in 2001. She teaches part-time at Vancouver Island University.

Tom Rachman, a novelist and journalist, was born in 1974 in England and raised in Vancouver. He studied cinema at the University of Toronto and journalism at Columbia University. Reporting and editing—for the *Associated Press*, then the *International Herald Tribune*—took him from New York to India to Japan and Egypt and around Europe. To write fiction full-time, he quit journalism and moved to Paris. His first novel, *The Imperfectionists* (2010), was an international bestseller, longlisted for the Giller Prize, and translated into twenty-five languages. Later books have been nominated for the Costa Prize, the Sky Arts Award, and the Edge Hill Prize, and appeared on "Best of the Year" lists in the *Globe and Mail*, *NPR*, the *Daily Mail*, and elsewhere. His fiction includes *The Rise & Fall of Great Powers* (2014), *Basket of Deplorables* (2017), and *The Italian Teacher* (2018). His latest novel, *The Imposters*, comes out in 2023. Rachman, who lives in London, tweets rarely and badly at @TomRachman.

ME Rogan is an award-winning magazine writer living in Toronto. A three-time gold medal winner at the National Magazine Awards, they took gold in the NMA's inaugural long-form feature-writing category for "Growing Up Trans" and again in 2022 for their most recent work, "Quitting America." Both articles appeared in *The Walrus*, Canada's premier literary magazine.

Rogan's work has appeared in *Esquire*, *GQ*, *SEED*, the *New York Times Magazine*, *The Best American Science Writing*, *Readers Digest*, *Best Canadian Essays*, *Toronto Life*, *Chatelaine*, *The Walrus*, the *National Post*, the *Globe and Mail*, and other publications.

Before launching into magazine writing, Rogan was a senior radio producer and on-air contributor at the Canadian Broadcasting Corporation.

Allan Stratton is the internationally acclaimed author of *Chanda's Secrets*, winner of over twenty-six awards and citations, including the American Library Association's Michael L Printz Honor Book, the Children's Africana Book Award, and *Booklist*'s Editor's Choice. The film adaptation *Life, Above All*, won the Francois Chalais Prize at the Cannes International Film Festival, 2010, and was South Africa's official entry for the 2011 Oscar for best foreign language film. Allan's other YA and children's novels include: *Chanda's Wars*, winner of the Young Adult Canadian Book Award, 2009; *Borderline* and *Leslie's Journal*, ALA Best Fiction; *The Grave Robber's Apprentice*, a Governor General's Award nominee and *Times of London* Book of the Week; *Curse of the Dream Witch*, the 2014 Canadian Library Association Best Book for Children Award; and *The Dogs*, winner of the 2015 Red Maple Award, ALA Quick Picks (USA) selection, Carnegie Medal (UK) longlist. His last novel, *The Way Back Home*, won Italy's 2019 Scelte di classe for Best YA and the MYRCA Award; was a Governor General's Award finalist and Red Maple Award runner-up; and was nominated for the Clip-Carnegie Medal.

Allan's play *Nurse Jane Goes to Hawaii* (1980), with over 350 North American productions, is one of the most produced plays in Canadian theatre history. His other plays, which include *Rexy!*, *Papers*, and *Bag Babies*, have variously won the Canadian Authors Association Award, the Dora Mavor Moore Award, the Chalmers Award, and been nominated for the Governor General's Award. Published in twenty-five countries, he lives in Toronto with his husband and two cats.

Sarmishta Subramanian is a writer and editor living in Toronto. She was editor-in-chief of the *Literary Review of Canada* and deputy editor of *The Walrus* at launch. She has been a senior editor at *Maclean's*, *Saturday Night*, the *National Post*, *Chatelaine*, and the *Toronto Star*, where she is executive features editor. Her work has appeared in many of those publications, and she has produced award-winning documentaries for the CBC. She was editor of *Best Canadian Essays 2020* (Biblioasis).

NOTABLE ESSAYS

Ken Babstock, "When Death is Preferable to Taxes."
The Walrus 18,3 (May 2021)

Cúagilákv (Jess Housty), "Thriving Together: Salmon, Berries, and People."
Hakai Magazine (April 27, 2021)

Adrienne Gruber, "Sea Monsters Revealed."
Event 50,1

Dan Hill, "'My pain was your pain': On Wrestling With My Racial Inheritance at a Moment of Great Reckoning."
Globe and Mail (February 6, 2021)

Anna Leventhal, "A Strong Family Resemblance."
Maisonneuve 79 (Spring 2021)

Ethan Lou, "A fistful of Bitcoins: How Wild West Frontier Myths Explain the Draw of Cryptocurrency."
Globe and Mail (October 16, 2021)

Richard Warnica, "Rothko at the Inauguration."
Hazlitt (December 6, 2021)

Ira Wells, "'Solutioning' Through Our 'Pain Points': The New
    Biz Speak, and Why So Many People Now Talk Like Tech
    CEOs."
Toronto Star (November 14, 2021)

PUBLICATIONS CONSULTED FOR THE 2023 EDITION

Aeon, Antigonish Review, Arc Poetry Magazine, Best Health Magazine, Brick, Canada's History, Canadian Notes & Queries, Dalhousie Review, [EDIT], Event, The Fiddlehead, filling Station, Geist, Globe and Mail, Grain, Granta, Hazlitt, Literary Review of Canada, Maisonneuve, The Malahat Review, The Nashwaak Review, The New Quarterly, New York Times, Newfoundland Quarterly, Prairie Fire, PRISM international, Queen's Quarterly, Quillette, Room, The Tyee, University of Toronto Quarterly, The Walrus

ACKNOWLEDGEMENTS

"Afghanistan, the Beautiful Land of Endless Suffering" by Jamaluddin Aram first appeared in the *Globe and Mail*. Reprinted by permission of the author.

"On Ageing Alone" by Sharon Butala first appeared in *The Walrus*. A version of this essay appeared in *This Strange Visible Air: Essays on Ageing and the Writing Life* by Sharon Butala (Freehand Books, 2021). Reprinted by permission of the author and publisher.

"The Sun Is Always in Your Eyes in Rexdale" by Kunal Chaudhary first appeared in *Spacing*. Reprinted by permission of the author.

"Blind Spots" by Christopher Cheung appeared in *The Tyee*. This essay first appeared in the *Toronto Star* as the Dalton Camp Award winner (FRIENDS, 2021). Reprinted by permission of the author and publisher.

"Genetic Mapping" by Emma Gilchrist first appeared in *Maisonneuve*. Reprinted by permission of the author.

ACKNOWLEDGEMENTS

"'Play Indians' Inflict Real Harm on Indigenous People" by Michelle Good first appeared in the *Globe and Mail*. Reprinted by permission of the author.

"We're All Teenagers Now" by Paul Howe first appeared in *Aeon*. Reprinted by permission of the author.

"Why the Filet-O-Fish is My Standard for Fast Food" by Jane Hu first appeared in the *New York Times*. Reprinted by permission of the author.

"Klein Bottle" by Heather Jessup first appeared in *Brick*. Reprinted by permission of the author.

"A Man, Without" by Chafic LaRochelle first appeared in *The Fiddlehead*. Reprinted by permission of the author.

"Toil and Trouble" by Stephen Marche first appeared in the *Literary Review of Canada*. Reprinted by permission of the author.

"That Other Place" by Kathy Page first appeared in *The New Quarterly*. Reprinted by permission of the author.

"Where Is Intellectual Courage in the Age of Twitter?" by Tom Rachman first appeared in the *Globe and Mail*. Reprinted by permission of the author.

"Quitting America" by ME Rogan first appeared in *The Walrus*. Reprinted by permission of the author.

"Rescuing the Radicalized Discourse on Sex and Gender: Part Two of a Three-Part Series" by Allan Stratton first appeared in *Quillette*. Reprinted by permission of the author.

ACKNOWLEDGEMENTS

"Going the Distance: How Covid Has Remapped Friendships" by Sarmishta Subramanian first appeared in *Best Health Magazine*. Reprinted by permission of the author.

Mireille Silcoff is the author of four books, including the award-winning story collection *Chez L'arabe*. She is a regular contributor to the *New York Times Magazine*, and was a Weekend culture columnist at the *National Post* for over a decade. Mireille is the founding editor of literary journal *Guilt & Pleasure Quarterly* and for many years, ran a raucous discussion salon in Toronto. She is currently finishing her next work, the book-length essay about our souls and our homes, called *On Interiors*. She lives in Montreal with her two young daughters.

Printed by Imprimerie Gauvin
Gatineau, Québec